EMERGENT STRATEGY

Shaping Change, Changing Worlds

EMERGENT STRATEGY

Shaping Change, Changing Worlds

by adrienne maree brown

© 2017 adrienne maree brown

ISBN: 978-1-84935-260-4
E-ISBN: 978-1-84935-261-1
Library of Congress Control Number: 2016941996

AK Press
370 Ryan Ave. #100
Chico, CA 95973
USA
www.akpress.org
akpress@akpress.org

AK Press
33 Tower St.
Edinburgh EH6 7BN
Scotland
www.akuk.com
ak@akedin.demon.co.uk

The above addresses would be delighted to provide you with the latest AK Press distribution catalog, which features books, pamphlets, zines, and stylish apparel published and/or distributed by AK Press. Alternatively, visit our websites for the complete catalog, latest news, and secure ordering.

Cover design by Herb Thornby
Interior design by Margaret Killjoy | birdsbeforethestorm.net
Printed in the USA

CONTENTS

I dedicate this book to the memory of Grace Lee Boggs, who opened the door to emergence and pushed me through, who taught me to keep listening and learning and having conversations. She said, "Transform yourself to transform the world."
I dedicate this book also to the memory of Charity Hicks, who saw all the interconnected patterns as clear as day. She said, "Wage love."

"This may only be a dream of mine, but I think it can be made real."
—Ella Baker

INTRODUCTION

First and foremost, thank you for opening this book. I hope you enjoy reading it as much as I have enjoyed living, learning, and gathering it.

Wherever you are beginning this, take a deep breath and notice how you feel in your body, and how the world around you feels.

Take a breath for the day you have had so far.

And a breath for this precious moment, which cannot be recreated.

Now, another for the day and night coming.

Here you are, in the cycle between the past and the future, choosing to spend your miraculous time in the exploration of how humans, especially those seeking to grow liberation and justice, can learn from the world around us how to best collaborate, how to shape change.[1]

As I am gathering and writing this book, there is a trail of ants moving along the ceiling of my room, and the sounds of a small jungle town coming in and out of the screened open windows, birds cawing, laughter, children's delight emerging from that, then tears. A car backfires and I flinch, a lizard

---

1   I've developed my ideas of "shaping change" in conversation with
     Octavia Butler's concept of "shaping God," which is introduced in
     the Earthseed verses of her *Parable of the Sower* (New York: Four Walls
     Eight Windows, 1993).

peeks at me from the door. It's been raining for a few days and the air feels thick.

I feel good, I've been meditating, picking up my yoga practice, biking the two miles to the beach when the sun comes out. Something is injured in my knee, but I am feeling alive against my limits.

I came to this edge of Mexico to pull a book together because, a few years ago, it was here, near this tiny portion of the massive ocean, that I began to realize how important emergent strategy, strategy for building complex patterns and systems of change through relatively small interactions, is to me—the potential scale of transformation that could come from movements intentionally practicing this adaptive, relational way of being, on our own and with others.

The waves drifting me towards and then away from the shore, seabirds of all kinds flocking over the salty blue, pelicans dropping down and scooping schools of tiny fish into their big mouths. Diving under the moving surface to see how everything humans leave in the water is repurposed as an ecosystem. Laying in a hammock and watching mosquito mamas approach me, wait for my attention to wander so they can feed on my blood.

I love the scene at the end of *The Matrix* where Neo sees everything in green-on-black code. Emergent strategy is a way that all of us can begin to see the world in life-code—awakening us to the sacred systems of life all around us. Many of us have been and are becoming students of these systems of life, wondering if in fact we can unlock some crucial understanding about our own humanity if we pay closer attention to this place we are from, the bodies we are in.

The world is full of beauty, magic, miracles, and patterns that induce wonder. This book is a collection of essays, speeches, spells, interviews, conversations, tools, profiles, and poems sharing my learning processes in the face of that wonder. You are basically holding a book of me saying, "Wow, everything's so amazing!" Or, "That's not wow… Why not go with the wow option?"

Emergence is one of the best concepts I have learned for discussing this wow, this wonder. *"Emergence is the way complex systems and patterns arise out of a multiplicity of relatively simple interactions."*[2]

It is another way of speaking about the connective tissue of all that exists—the way, the Tao, the force, change, God/dess, life. Birds flocking, cells splitting, fungi whispering underground.

Emergence emphasizes critical connections over critical mass, building authentic relationships, listening with all the senses of the body and the mind.

With our human gift of reasoning, we have tried to control or overcome the emergent processes that are our own nature, the processes of the planet we live on, and the universe we call home. The result is crisis at each scale we are aware of, from our deepest inner moral sensibilities to the collective scale of climate and planetary health and beyond, to our species in relation to space and time.

The crisis is everywhere, massive massive massive.

And we are small.

But emergence notices the way small actions and connections create complex systems, patterns that become ecosystems and societies. Emergence is our inheritance as a part of this universe; it is how we change. Emergent strategy is how we intentionally change in ways that grow our capacity to embody the just and liberated worlds we long for.

A few words on what this book is and is not

I am offering this content as a cluster of thoughts in development, observations of existing patterns, and questions of how we apply the brilliance of the world around us to our efforts to coexist in and with this world as humans, particularly for those of us seeking to transform the crises of our time, to turn our legacy towards harmony.

---

2   Nick Obolensky, *Complex Adaptive Leadership: Embracing Paradox and Uncertainty* (Burlington, VT: Gower, 2014).

This book is for people who want to radically change the world.[3] To apply natural order and our love of life to the ways we create the next world. To tap into the most ancient systems and patterns for wisdom as we build tomorrow.

This book is not one that will teach you all about hard science, as I am not a scientist. As Octavia Butler said, "I would never have been a good scientist—my attention span was too short for that."

My style is more "Ooh ah wow how??" than "Empirical data proves that..." I am writing this book primarily for other people like myself, who crinkle our brows and lean away when someone starts speaking math, who fall asleep almost immediately when attempting to read nonfiction, but who get spun into wonder about the natural world and want to know things, who feel and know more than we can say or explain, and want to know how knowing those things can transform the ways we approach changing the world.

I'm sure there are science people who could write a contrarian book to anything in here.[4] The natural world actually supports any worldview—competitive, powerless, isolationist, violent.

For instance, humans so far have generally deified and aligned with the "king" of the jungle or forest—lions, tigers, bears. And yet so many of these creatures, for all their isolated ferocity and alpha power, are going extinct. While a major cause of that extinction is our human impact, there is something to be said for adaptation, the adaptation of small, collaborative species. Roaches and ants and deer and fungi and bacteria and viruses and bamboo and eucalyptus and squirrels and vultures and mice and mosquitos and dandelions and so many other more collaborative life forms continue to proliferate, survive, grow. Sustain.

---

3   "Radical simply means 'grasping things at the root.'"—Angela Davis, "Let Us All Rise Together" Address, Spelman College, reprinted in *Women, Culture and Politics* (New York, Random House, 1989).

4   If that's you, then yay! I bet you're hella smart—help get us all free!

I want to understand how we humans do that—how we earn a place on this precious planet, get in the "right relationship" with it.[5] So I am focusing on the ways creatures and ecosystems function together in and with the natural world.

I am open to critiques of course, if they are offered in the spirit of collective liberation. Staying focused on our foundational miraculous nature is actually very hard work in our modern culture of deconstruction. We are socialized to see what is wrong, missing, off, to tear down the ideas of others and uplift our own. To a certain degree, our entire future may depend on learning to listen, listen without assumptions or defenses. So I am open to hearing what doesn't work about this book, as long as you promise to stay open to what does work.

We all learn differently, and this book favors those who learn like me, through inspiration, through late-night conversations, personal revelations, experience, and reflection. I hope it will inspire and engage your interest in complex sciences, and in being of a miraculous world.

"Exercise your human mind as fully as possible, knowing it is only an exercise. Build beautiful artifacts, solve problems, explore the secrets of the physical universe, savor the input from all the senses, feel the joy and sorrow, the laughter, the empathy, compassion and tote the emotional memory in your travel bag."
—Ryan Power, *Waking Life*

This is not a book to displace all the strategic processes in play in social justice movements, or to discount the work

---

5   "The mountains, streams, valleys, oceans, deserts, and all things are related to our thoughts and actions. All things are in relationship with each other."—Jasmine Wallace, a Tsalagi (Cherokee) medicine woman, https://certified.naturallygrown.org/producers/4166.

that has happened up until now—there have been effective movements towards justice and liberation throughout the history of human existence—I am thrilled by how humans have continuously stood up against our own weaknesses. I think throughout history we have done our best given what we knew, and we will continue to do so. I also know that there are so many brilliant strategists out there who turn data into action and policy, and I respect that work. I see this offering as a noticing that can shape our next steps, as more water joining the river. And as a way to get aware of what we have learned so far, so that we can move forward from there, instead of repeating lessons we have already learned.

While my default position is wonder, I am not without critique, disappointment, frustration, and even depression when I contemplate humanity. Especially our social justice movements, where my expectations are (foolishly) higher. I promise to be honest about the ways that those aspects of personal movement crisis show up in my longing and searching for other ways of being.

Octavia Butler, one of the cornerstones of my awareness of emergent strategy, spoke of the fatal human flaw as a combination of hierarchy and intelligence.[6] We are brilliant at survival, but brutal at it. We tend to slip out of togetherness the way we slip out of the womb, bloody and messy and surprised to be alone. And clever—able to learn with our whole bodies the ways of this world.

My hope is that this content will deepen and soften that intelligence such that we can align our behavior, our structures and our movements with our visions of justice and liberation, and give those of us co-creating the future more options for working with each other and embodying the things we fight for—dignity, collective power, love, generative conflict, and community.

I will be satisfied if this book sparks conversations, new practices, and projects where people keep noticing, observing,

---

6   Octavia Butler, *Dawn* (New York: Grand Central Publishing, 1987).

and learning about emergence and liberation. If people see their experimental work affirmed by this content. And if I hear of people's self and collective transformation journeys related to emergent strategy, whether people use that exact terminology or not. I hope it is part of our (r)evolutionary journey.

I hope that this book is clear enough that people feel free to play with all of these observations and their own, add to it, discard what doesn't serve, and keep innovating. I don't want to be the owner of this, just a joyful conduit.

Throughout the book I weave together thoughts and theories I have learned in the past decades of study and obsession with original content, tools, spells, poems, examples, lists, assessments—everything I can think of that could be helpful for those interested in this work.

As I was finishing the book it felt like it was missing something. I realized that it was because the way I have learned about emergent strategy is in conversation with others, so I asked a bunch of people I consider to be teachers in my life to get in conversation with me. And as their words poured in, in poems and quotes and stories and testimonials, all of a sudden the book became really alive and exciting to me. It also grew to nearly five-hundred pages. I slowed down and started weaving and listening. Now you get to hear from a variety of people who are doing emergent strategy work—in their own words, in hybrid interview/conversations, in love stories and moments of wow. Some of this content is in these pages, and some of it is on the Emergent Strategy Ideation Institute site.[7]

The book can be engaged nonlinearly! There is an assessment section, you can start there and let that determine where you dive in. You can just go straight to the tools at the end and start facilitating and experimenting with them. Or you can start with a review of the principles and elements of

---

7   Emergent Strategy Ideation Institute's website can be found at http://www.alliedmedia.org/esii.

emergent strategy, which are in conversation with each other and can stand alone or cluster.

You can read the book with others, assess each other and assess the groups and circles you move in. Come up with new words and new observations for all of this, notice how it connects and echoes other theoretical frameworks. Underline everything that moves you and then give it to someone younger than you. Come up with workshops and retreats around this work. Take it, run, go, grow, innovate, emerge.

You can also just like the idea of this book. I often like an idea that I don't have time or attention to fully engage. I won't be mad! I believe we are all actually already aware of these things, we just have the volume turned down. May this serve as a turn up of our awareness of our place in the miraculous.

There are a million paths into the future, and many of them can be transformative for the whole.

The Beginning of My Obsession

We have lived through a good half century of individualistic linear organizing (led by charismatic individuals or budget-building institutions), which intends to reform or revolutionize society, but falls back into modeling the oppressive tendencies against which we claim to be pushing. Some of those tendencies are seeking to assert one right way or one right strategy. Many align with the capitalistic belief that constant growth and critical mass is the only way to create change, even if they don't use that language.

There are new strategies emerging, or being remembered—many would describe this as a shift from a masculine to feminine (or patriarchal to feminist) leadership. I see that, and I think it is also about something beyond all of our binaries—evolving in relationship with our hierarchical tendency.

At this point in my life, I am not against hierarchy. I notice hierarchies in my life and attention all the time, inside my own preferences for whom I spend my waking hours with and how I like to spend my time. I also deeply value experience and natural affinity for things—I am oriented towards healing and not math, so I don't offer myself up to create budgets for people. I follow other people's leadership around math, I offer leadership around healing, which comes more naturally to me. That give and take creates room for micro-hierarchies in a collaborative environment.

One of my favorite questions today is: How do we turn our collective full-bodied intelligence towards collaboration, if that is the way we will survive?

My favorite life forms right now are dandelions and mushrooms—the resilience in these structures, which we think of as weeds and fungi, the incomprehensible scale, the clarity of identity, excites me. I love to see the way mushrooms can take substances we think of as toxic, and process them as food, or that dandelions spread not only themselves but their community structure, manifesting their essential qualities (which include healing and detoxifying the human body) to proliferate and thrive in a new environment. The resilience of these life forms is that they evolve while maintaining core practices that ensure their survival.

A mushroom *is* a toxin-transformer, a dandelion *is* a community of healers waiting to spread... What are we as humans, what is our function in the universe?

One thing I have observed: When we are engaged in acts of love, we humans are at our best and most resilient. The love in romance that makes us want to be better people, the love of children that makes us change our whole lives to meet their needs, the love of family that makes us drop everything to take care of them, the love of community that makes us work tirelessly with broken hearts.

Perhaps humans' core function is love. Love leads us to observe in a much deeper way than any other emotion. I think of how delightful it is to see something new in my lovers' faces, something they may only know from inside as a feeling.

If love were the central practice of a new generation of organizers and spiritual leaders, it would have a massive impact on what was considered organizing. If the goal was to increase the love, rather than winning or dominating a constant opponent, I think we could actually imagine liberation from constant oppression. We would suddenly be seeing everything we do, everyone we meet, not through the tactical eyes of war, but through eyes of love. We would see that there's no such thing as a blank canvas, an empty land or a new idea—but everywhere there is complex, ancient, fertile ground full of potential.

We would organize with the perspective that there is wisdom and experience and amazing story in the communities we love, and instead of starting up new ideas/organizations all the time, we would want to listen, support, collaborate, merge, and grow through fusion, not competition.

We would understand that the strength of our movement is in the strength of our relationships, which could only be measured by their depth. Scaling up would mean going deeper, being more vulnerable and more empathetic.

What does depth require from us, from me? In my longing for depth I have been re-rooting in the earth, in myself and my creativity, in my community, in my spiritual practices, honing in on work that is not only meaningful but feels joyful, listening with less and less judgment to the ideas and efforts of others, having visions that are long term.

Another part of walking this path has been the practice of humility—enough humility to learn, to be taught, to have teachers. As a military brat, I've always rebelled against anyone I perceived as an authority. It's been hard and rewarding work to relinquish some of that resistance in order to let wisdom in.

The Sufi poet Hafiz said, "How do I listen to others? As if everyone were my Teacher, speaking to me (Her) cherished last words."[8]

I am listening now with all of my senses, as if the whole universe might exist just to teach me more about love. I listen

---

8   Hazif, *The Gift: Poems by Hafiz, the Great Sufi Master*, trans. Daniel Ladinsky (New York: Penguin Books, 1999).

to strangers, I listen to random invitations, I listen to criticisms, I listen to my body, I listen to my creativity and to the artists who inspire me, I listen to elders, I listen to my dreams and the books I am reading. I notice that the more I pay attention, the more I see order, clear messages, patterns, and invitations in the small or seemingly random things that happen in my life.

In all these ways, I meditate on love.

This practice lets me connect to the part of myself that is divine, aligned with the universe, and the place within myself where I can be a conduit for spiritual truth—I don't know what else to call it. What comes forth, as lessons and realizations and beliefs—doesn't feel political, or even about organizing. It feels like spirit leading me to the truth.

Things like:

- The less I engage in gossip, the less I harbor suspicion, the more space I find within myself for miraculous experiences.
- When I fear the universe, I fear myself. When I love and am in awe of the universe, I love and am in awe of myself.[9] Imagine then, the power when I align with the universe.
- Nothing is required of me more than being, and creating. Simultaneously being present with who I am, who we are as a species…and creating who we must become, and within that who *I* must become.

When these truths come to me, it reminds me of how so many past leaders have humbled themselves, or been forced—through prison sentences, exile, or other punitive measures—to live simple lives, spending time in prayer and

---

9   Though I wrote this before the Queen released Her album, I would be pleased if you thought I was referencing the lyric "love god herself," from "Don't Hurt Yourself" on Beyoncé's masterpiece *Lemonade* (2015).

meditation and reflection. It reminds me that they all seem to have this solid core of truth within themselves that cannot be shaken by external pressures. Those truths resonate with me when I read or hear about them, even without the context of their whole spiritual journey. But I know that to truly understand, to truly be able to transform myself and develop that own unflappable core, I cannot vicariously live their spiritual lessons: I must walk my own path.

Our generation must walk the spiritual path that is available to us only in this time, with its own unique combination of wisdom and creation.

I think there are many ways to find that simple path within ourselves, and I think that those of us who wish to see a truly, radically different world must demand of ourselves the possibility that we are called to lead not from right to left, or from minority to majority, but from spirit towards liberation.

So I suppose it is time to come out as a spiritual leader, in my own way.

Which means—everyone is my teacher.

"You weren't starving before you got here. You were born full."
—Chani Nicholas

To write this book, I have had to get intimate with what I don't know, with my fears and doubts, with my restlessness. I was very young the first time I felt this restlessness, this sense that how things are isn't right, isn't enough, is empty even. Even as a child this sense made me nauseous, like dancing around a black hole, praying it is a portal and not a nothingness. As I get older, I understand that it is the unknown, and it is where the most exciting parts of life happen.

This is my leap into the unknown.

What is Emergent Strategy?

"Emergence is the way complex systems and patterns arise out of a multiplicity of relatively simple interactions"—I will repeat these words from Nick Obolenksy throughout this book because they are the clearest articulation of emergence that I have come across. In the framework of emergence, the whole is a mirror of the parts. Existence is fractal—the health of the cell is the health of the species and the planet.

There are examples of emergence everywhere.

Birds don't make a plan to migrate, raising resources to fund their way, packing for scarce times, mapping out their pit stops. They feel a call in their bodies that they must go, and they follow it, responding to each other, each bringing their adaptations.

There is an art to flocking: staying separate enough not to crowd each other, aligned enough to maintain a shared direction, and cohesive enough to always move towards each other. (Responding to destiny together.) Destiny is a calling that creates a beautiful journey.

Emergence is beyond what the sum of its parts could even imagine.

A group of caterpillars or nymphs might not see flight in their future, but it's inevitable.

It's destiny.

Oak trees don't set an intention to listen to each other better, or agree to hold tight to each other when the next storm comes. Under the earth, always, they reach for each other, they grow such that their roots are intertwined and create a system of strength that is as resilient on a sunny day as it is in a hurricane.

Dandelions don't know whether they are a weed or a brilliance. But each seed can create a field of dandelions. We are invited to be that prolific. And to return fertility to the soil around us.

Cells may not know civilization is possible. They don't amass as many units as they can sign up to be the same.

No—they grow until they split, complexify. Then they interact and intersect and discover their purpose—I am a lung cell! I am a tongue cell!—and they serve it. And they die. And what emerges from these cycles are complex organisms, systems, movements, societies.

Nothing is wasted, or a failure. Emergence is a system that makes use of everything in the iterative process. It's all data.

Octavia Butler said, "civilization is to groups what intelligence is to individuals. It is a means of combining the intelligence of many to achieve ongoing group adaptation."[10]

She also said "all that you touch you change / all that you change, changes you."[11] We are constantly impacting and changing our civilization—each other, ourselves, intimates, strangers. And we are working to transform a world that is, by its very nature, in a constant state of change.

Janine Benyus, a student of biomimicry, says "Nature/Life would always create conditions conducive to life."[12] She tells of a radical fringe of scientists who are realizing that natural selection isn't individual, but mutual—that species only survive if they learn to be in community.

How can we, future ancestors, align ourselves with the most resilient practices of emergence as a species?

Many of us have been socialized to understand that constant growth, violent competition, and critical mass are the ways to create change. But emergence shows us that adaptation and evolution depend more upon critical, deep, and authentic connections, a thread that can be tugged for support and resilience. The quality of connection between the nodes in the patterns.

Dare I say love.

And we know how to connect—we long for it.

---

10   Octavia Butler, *Parable of the Sower*.

11   Ibid.

12   Janine M. Benyus, *Biomimicry: Innovation Inspired by Nature* (New York: Harper Perennial, 2002).

Octavia Butler	**(amb)**
All successful life is	(Fractal)
Adaptable,	(Adaptive)
Opportunistic,	(Nonlinear/Iterative)
Tenacious,	(Resilient/Transformative Justice)
Interconnected, and	(Interdependent/Decentralized)
Fecund.	(Creates More Possibilities)
Understand this.	(Scholarship, Reflection)
Use it.	(Practice/Experiment)
Shape God.	(Intention)

Together we must move like waves. Have you observed the ocean? The waves are not the same over and over—each one is unique and responsive. The goal is not to repeat each other's motion, but to respond in whatever way feels right in *your* body. The waves we create are both continuous and a one-time occurrence. We must notice what it takes to respond well. How it feels to be in a body, in a whole—separate, aligned, cohesive. Critically connected.

I would call our work to change the world "science fictional behavior"—being concerned with the way our actions and beliefs now, today, will shape the future, tomorrow, the next generations.

We are excited by what we can create, we believe it is possible to create the next world.

We believe.

For me this might be because I was born to a trekkie—meaning one who watches *Star Trek*. Obsessively.

My dad watched *Star Trek* in a way that seems logical to me now. He watched this "post-racist" narrative as Black man from the deep south bringing multiracial children into a racist world—eyes wide, faith bubbling up.

We all watched it together, as his military career took our family from place to place. My parents intentionally took us away from the United States for our early years and I think they believed that by the time we came back here things would have changed on the race front.

That didn't happen, and the time came to return to the US—my father was stationed in Georgia. I think what I experienced there, the casual and constant presence of white supremacy, the knee-jerk assessments of my intelligence and humanity, is one of the foundational catalysts for my study of sci fi, apocalypse and post-apocalypse, emergence and complexity.

I thought then, and I think now: This can't be all. No one survives this way, not long term. This can't be the purpose of our species, to constantly identify each other as "other," build walls between us, and engage in both formal and informal wars against each other's bodies.

I felt, and feel, miraculous. It's confusing to feel so miraculous when so many people hate my skin and my history.

I see the miraculous in others—even those who hate me have heartbeats, and, I generally assume, have people they love. Why can't they love me? Should I love them anyway? How can I hold these massive contradictions?

I started reading sci fi obsessively, looking for options, for other worlds where I wasn't dismissed as an idealist or an inferior.

On that path I discovered Octavia Butler. Decades before my birth, she was working these same edges in her heart, pendulum swinging between curiosity, possibility, and hopelessness. Because if we can't articulate more viable futures, and adapt, our human future is pretty hopeless.

Octavia wrote novels with young Black women protagonists meeting aliens, surviving apocalypse, evolving into vampires, becoming telepathic networks, time traveling to reckon with slave-owning ancestors. Woven throughout her work are two things: 1) a coherent visionary exploration of humanity and 2) emergent strategies for being better humans.

A visionary exploration of humanity includes imagination. Octavia spent her life working through complex ideas of the future on behalf of humans.

As long as we operate in time the way we currently do—remembering the past, observing and acting in the present, imagining the future—there will be divergent paths that are moving in and out of alignment, in and out of conflict. Imagination is shaped by our entire life experience, our socialization, the concepts we are exposed to, where we fall in the global hierarchies of society.

Our ideas of right and wrong shift with time—right now it's clear to me that something is wrong if it hurts this planet. But if we don't claim the future, that sense of loyalty to earth, of environmentalism, could become outdated. Kenny Bailey[13] helped me understand this—that justice, rights,

---

13   Kenny Bailey is one of the founders of the Design Studio for

things we take for granted, are not permanent. Once there were kings and queens all over the earth. Someday we might speak of presidents and CEOs in past tense only.

It is so important that we fight for the future, get into the game, get dirty, get experimental. How do we create and proliferate a compelling vision of economies and ecologies that center humans and the natural world over the accumulation of material?

We embody. We learn. We release the idea of failure, because it's all data.

But first we imagine.

We are in an imagination battle.[14]

Trayvon Martin and Mike Brown and Renisha McBride and so many others are dead because, in some white imagination, they were dangerous. And that imagination is so respected that those who kill, based on an imagined, racialized fear of Black people, are rarely held accountable.

Imagination has people thinking they can go from being poor to a millionaire as part of a shared American dream. Imagination turns Brown bombers into terrorists and white bombers into mentally ill victims. Imagination gives us borders, gives us superiority, gives us race as an indicator of capability. I often feel I am trapped inside someone else's imagination, and I must engage my own imagination in order to break free.

All of this imagining, in the poverty of our current system, is heightened because of scarcity economics. There isn't enough, so we need to hoard, enclose, divide, fence up, and prioritize resources and people.

Innovation, a Boston-based artistic research and development outfit that serves civil society.

14 The goddess-writer Claudia Rankine (author of the award-winning book, *Citizen*) and Terry Marshall (of Intelligent Mischief, a creative intelligent design lab) each speak of this in different ways in their work. They have both inspired me and transformed my understanding of the importance of creative work.

We have to imagine beyond those fears. We have to ideate—imagine and conceive—together.

We must imagine new worlds that transition ideologies
and norms, so that no one sees Black people as murderers, or
Brown people as terrorists and aliens, but all of us as potential
cultural and economic innovators. This is a time-travel exercise for the heart. This is collaborative ideation—what are the
ideas that will liberate all of us?

The more people that collaborate on that ideation, the
more that people will be served by the resulting world(s).

Science fiction is simply a way to practice the future together. I suspect that is what many of you are up to, practicing futures together, practicing justice together, living
into new stories. It is our right and responsibility to create a
new world.

What we pay attention to grows, so I'm thinking about
how we grow what we are all imagining and creating into
something large enough and solid enough that it becomes a
tipping point.

Ursula Le Guin recently said, "It's up to authors to spark
the imagination of their readers and to help them envision
alternatives to how we live."[15]

I agree with her. As Toni Cade Bambara has taught us, we
must make just and liberated futures irresistible.[16] We are all
the protagonists of what might be called the great turning,
the change, the new economy, the new world.

And I think it is healing behavior, to look at something
so broken and see the possibility and wholeness in it. That's
how I work as a healer: when a body is between my hands, I
let wholeness pour through. We are all healers too—we are
creating possibilities, because we are seeing a future full of
wholeness.

---

15 From the November 2014 acceptance speech for the National Book
   Foundation's medal for Distinguished Contribution to American
   Letters.
16 From interview with Kay Bonetti, 1982.

I suspect this is, in part, because we are practicing emergent strategies.

My mentor Grace Lee Boggs first raised the concept of emergence with us in Detroit after reading Margaret Wheatley's work about biomimicry and mycelium magic.[17] Grace started asking us what our movements would look like if we focused on critical connections instead of critical mass.

We need each other. I love the idea of shifting from "mile wide inch deep" movements to "inch wide mile deep" movements that schism the existing paradigm.[18]

Now, I've said what emergence is. *Strategy* is a military term simply meaning a plan of action towards a goal.[19]

In our movements for social change (and in every other space I've ever been in), we generally use the word "strategy" in a positive sense. We say, "oh wow s/he's so *strategic!*," and we mean that this person is smart, calculating, practical—a winner! But the word is actually not that discerning. Horrible, racist, sexist, ableist, patriarchal, outdated, inflexible plans can be pitched as strategic.

We must be more precise.

Emergent strategies are ways for humans to practice complexity and grow the future through relatively simple interactions. This juxtaposition of emergence and strategy was what made the most sense to me when I was trying to explain the kind of leadership I see in Octavia's books.

---

17 Margaret Wheatley, *Leadership and the New Science* (Oakland: Berrett-Koehler Publishers, 1992).

18 I first experienced this "inch wide mile deep" language when it was used to speak about the work of the Detroit Future Youth program at Allied Media Projects. I've since heard it used to speak of work that prioritizes depth in community organizing, and understands that meaningful scale depends on deep transformative work, rather than surface widespread work.

19 Confession: As the first daughter of a colonel in the US Army, I cut my political teeth in conversation with my father, who served as the Chief of War Plans while I was in college.

It isn't just that her protagonists are Black, female, or young leaders... Or maybe it is because of all of those things: who leads matters. But what I noticed is that her leaders are adaptive—riding change like dolphins ride the ocean. Adaptive but also intentional, like migrating birds who know how to get where they're going even when a storm pushes them a hundred miles off course.

Humans? Some of us are surviving, following, flocking—but some of us are trying to imagine where we are going as we fly. That is radical imagination.

Octavia's protagonists were also interdependent, often polyamorous. I suspect that Octavia understood from her own feelings of loneliness, desire, and pleasure that the personal is political, and that pleasure evokes change—perhaps more than shame. More precisely, where shame makes us freeze and try to get really small and invisible, pleasure invites us to move, to open, to grow.

At this point, we have all of the information we need to create a change; it isn't a matter of facts. It's a matter of longing, having the will to imagine and implement something else. We are living in the ancestral imagination of others, with their longing for safety and abundance, a longing that didn't include us, or included us as enemy, fright, other.

Octavia played with what emerged from a Black woman or girl—what longings, what pleasure, what communities and connections, what philosophies and divinities. The strategies that played out in Octavia's books included adaptability and interdependence—often through the practice of repeated vulnerability.

Right now there is an organization called Black Organizing for Leadership and Dignity (BOLD), which is cultivating a safe space for Black leaders to practice being vulnerable, being in mutual support, with a goal of countering the usual model of leader isolation.[20] We all need a place where we can

---

20   BOLD is a national Leadership Training Program designed to help rebuild Black (African-American, Caribbean, African, Afro-Latino) social

weep and be held and feel our feelings and figure out how those feelings can direct our next evolution.

I am now part of the training team for BOLD, and I can honestly say that after a period of movement heartbreak and disillusionment, the focus on love and relationship at BOLD is what brought me back to justified and tangible hope, opening up inside me the generosity of time and gifts that is necessary for movements to grow. I wanted to be a part of movement again because it was a pleasure to be in the Black spaces that BOLD was creating.

What amazes me is that, in the space of such constant Black trauma, we get together and celebrate and love on each other, we laugh, we find the pleasure of community, of interdependence. It feels good together.

Octavia's leaders were also decentralized, and they were generative—resilience and solutions came from that decentralization; the collective response was possible because no one person held the power.

Ferguson, Baltimore, Minneapolis, Chicago show us the power of individuals willing to act without a single leader, and their leaderfull examples are inspiring others to stand up in real time, offline and online, to change legislation and perception.

Octavia was concerned with scale—understanding that what happens at the interpersonal level is a way to understand the whole of society. In many of her books, she shows us how radical ideas spread through conversation, questions, one to one interactions. Social movements right now are also fractal, practicing at a small scale what we most want to see at the universal level. No more growth or scaling up before actually learning through experience.

Rather than narrowing into one path forward, Octavia's leaders were creating more and more possibilities. Not one

---

justice infrastructure in order to organize Black communities more effectively and to re-center Black leadership in the US social justice movement. More information available at www.boldblackorganizing.org.

perfect path forward, but an abundance of futures, of ways to manage resources together, to be brilliant together.

In trying to place Octavia into a context that non-sci fi people could understand, I kept finding resonance in emergence and complex sciences, the ideas that Grace had brought onto my radar. I started to pay more attention to the magic of the world, the small collective creatures who were humble and abundant and resilient.

And now I have become obsessed with how we can be movements like flocks of birds, underground power like whispering mushrooms, the seashell representation of a galactic vision for justice—small patterns that avoid useless predation, spread lessons, and proliferate change.

Emergent strategies let us practice, in every possible way, the world we want to see.

So, ok, but what EXACTLY is emergent strategy?

Emergent Strategy:

- was, initially, a way of describing the adaptive and relational leadership model found in the work of Black science fiction writer Octavia Butler (and others).
- then it grew into plans of action, personal practices and collective organizing tools that account for constant change and rely on the strength of relationship for adaptation. With a crush on biomimicry and permaculture.

Biomimetics or **biomimicry** is the imitation of the models, systems, and elements of nature for the purpose of solving complex human problems.

Permaculture is a system of agricultural and social design principles centered around simulating or directly utilizing the patterns and features observed in natural ecosystems.

- which evolved into strategies for organizers building movements for justice and liberation that leverage relatively simple interactions to create complex patterns, systems, and transformations—including adaptation, interdependence and decentralization, fractal awareness, resilience and transformative justice, nonlinear and iterative change, creating more possibilities.
- and now it's like…ways for humans to practice being in right relationship to our home and each other, to practice complexity, and grow a compelling future together through relatively simple interactions. Emergent strategy is how we intentionally change in ways that grow our capacity to embody the just and liberated worlds we long for.
- and maybe, if I'm honest, it's a philosophy for how to be in harmony and love, in and with the world.

a complex movement

over and over again
it becomes known
the peace we seek
is seeking us
the joy a full bud
awaiting our attention
justice in our hands
longing to be practiced
the whole world
learning
from within
this thrilling mote in the universe
laboratory
labyrinth
internalize demands
you are the one

you are waiting for
externalize love
bind us together into
a greater self
a complex movement
a generative abundance
an embodied evolution
learn to be here
critique is a seductress
her door is always open
so what if you get some
we are going further
past reform, to wonder
this requires comprehension
that cannot fit in words
out beyond our children
beyond the end of time
there is a ceaseless cycle
a fractal of sublime
and we come to create it
to soil our hands and faces
loving loving and loving
ourselves, and all our places

Lineage of Emergent Strategy

Lineage is both important for me to name, and impossible to track. I've come across these concepts in so many ways and places, primarily in the natural world, in my own body, in the development of my nibblings,[21] in movements (including the Movement for Black Lives and Occupy), in stories of how my paternal grandmother survived and created life in Pendleton, South Carolina, in stories of how my ancestors survived slavery.

---

21 Yes! A gender-neutral term for the children of my siblings, learned from Chicago-based healer/writer Tanuja Jagernauth.

Every time I have worked with Indigenous communities that have been able to sustain their cultural practices through the onslaught of colonialism and imperialism, as I listen, I hear emergent strategy—being in right relationship with the natural world, learning from the ways change and resilience happen throughout this entire interconnected complex system. Some Indigenous and First Nations friends and teachers have patiently listened to my "discoveries" around being humble in the face of the unknown, listening closely to all that is within and beyond our human ways of knowing. Honoring the changes that come through longing, honoring the very small things that create the largest shifts in the world.

I am the first child of two people who created a large shift for themselves from small actions, actions of love, weighted with the context of their time—a Black man and white woman finding lifelong, life-changing commitment in the context of white supremacy and racism, external and internal. And it was quick—a noticing each other, a flirting without words, talking, laughing, and, four months later, eloping. I showed up a year and a half later. Love overcame racist socialization, creating more possibilities between two people who had been taught the other was dangerous.

After family, there is a certain convergence of thinkers and conversations that has sharpened this particular set of concepts into something I could name and share. Most of this particular lineage happened on worn down couches and over kitchen tables in Detroit from 2008 to 2014.

In 1992, Margaret Wheatley published a book called *Leadership and the New Science*, based on her work with organizations and leaders on what is effective, through a lens of quantum physics, biology, and chaos theory. Her key learnings were that:

- everything is about relationships, critical connections;

- chaos is an essential process that we need to engage;
- the sharing of information is fundamental for organizational success; and
- vision is an invisible field that binds us together, emerging from relationships and chaos and information.

Wheatley has continued developing her thinking on how transformation happens, how communities learn and evolve. She has published a series of books, in which she explores and shares her learning—including how we listen to each other, and what communities around the world are doing to generate life, to generate cooperation and future together. When we met and worked together on a gathering of organizers in Detroit, I got the sense that she's a little over *Leadership*, so I encourage you to read it for the references—it is a foundational text—and then read everything else she is working on.

Grace Lee Boggs, Detroit-based American revolutionary, my late mentor and friend, read *Leadership* and began to incorporate some of the ideas into speeches and her own writing in the last decade of her one-hundred year, one-hundred day life. As a thinker, I would say Grace was a voracious, efficient beast, and philosophy was her hunting ground. She stayed curious and relevant until the end, asking metaphysical questions on her deathbed. And she was usually ahead of her time—she was creating visionary fiction with Bunyan Bryant in the 1970s.[22]

During the years of our mentorship and friendship, Grace would sit in her armchair and encourage everyone who came through her doors to develop as an organic intellectual who could take these concepts into daily life and community work.

---

22 "Visionary fiction" is a term coined by my *Octavia's Brood: Science Fiction from Social Justice Movements* co-editor Walidah Imarisha to describe the work of people who use fiction to advance justice and liberation.

Grace taught me dialectical humanism—the cycle of collective transformation of beliefs that occurs as we gather new information and experiences, meaning that, over time, we can understand and hold a position we previously believed to be wrong.[23]

In Grace's work, that cycle of transformation was foundational, something to cultivate in young people, in communities. In addition, she resonated with Wheatley's idea that critical connections are more important in a long-term transformation process than critical mass.

Relationships are everything.

Invincible/ill Weaver, a Detroit-based artist-organizer, heard about the book and concepts from Grace, and became a student of emergence, naming their music and media work after the concept and generating an award-winning multi-media interactive album/project called Complex Movements[24] around these and other concepts at the intersection of complex science and social justice.

I was reading Black, science fiction writer Octavia Butler's work over and over during that time. I was also visiting and eventually moving to Detroit, in large part due to my relationship with ill. As I've mentioned, I was looking for language and frameworks to use when exploring the kind of leadership Butler's protagonists practiced, and found them in conversations with ill and Grace about emergence—interdependence, iteration, being in relationship with constantly changing conditions, fractals.

---

23 "Organic intellectuals" comes from Antonio Gramsci and refers to intellectuals outside of traditional academic institutions, intellectuals who develop organically in counter relationship to the dominant culture. For more on Grace's concept of "dialectical humanism"—and its relationship to Karl Marx's dialectical materialism—see the Boggs Center website at http://www.boggscenter.org/.

24 Invincible should write a book about emergence—they do much more rigorous research on the science of things than I seem capable of. For more about the amazing work of Complex Movements check out https://emergencemedia.org/pages/complex-movements.

Emergence, particularly as it applies to change, was a thrilling match.

ill and I now have a work soulmateship—they are family, a chosen sibling, an idea confidante. Detroit's movement and arts scenes are actually a complex network of such familial relationships, cultivated through sharing resources, loving the city, and conversing as we learn together. I am a nomad who also feels rooted here because of this network.

Wheatley's work speaks of relationship—the depth of relationship between the individuals in a system determines the strength of the system. Butler, Wheatley, ill, Grace, myself, and many others have been growing a strong system of relationships for considering emergence as a game-changing approach to movement work.

Ok, But Who Are You?

Right. I'm adrienne maree brown. I am an auntie, sister, daughter, woe,[25] writer, facilitator, coach, mentor, mediator, pleasure activist, sci-fi scholar, doula, healer, tarot reader, witch, cheerleader, singer, philosopher, queer Black multiracial lover of life living in Detroit.

For this book, I am drawing most heavily on my facilitation, mediation, and coaching experiences—I have been facilitating social justice movement work formally since 2001, and before that, in high school and college, I did student organizing in which I often found myself in what I later came to understand as the facilitation role. Inside of that work I have been asked to mediate everything from organizational beef to break-ups, and have coached people through personal and professional transformation along the way.

---

25   I learned *woe* from the artist/rapper Drake, and I am deeply grateful for it. Actually, I owe gratitude to the Toronto rapper and producer Devontée who uses it to refer to his crew—who are always "working on excellence." It passed from him to fellow Canadian rapper Drake before I picked up on it. I use this term all the time and thank these men profusely.

I have supported environmental, food, reproductive, gender, economic, and other justice work over the years. At times, I worked formally in organizations that do harm reduction work with active drug users and sex workers, voter organizing at the national level, food justice work in Detroit, and nonviolent direct-action training, primarily supporting Indigenous peoples and other communities directly impacted by climate crisis. I also supported the second US Social Forum as a facilitator. I've held a variety of titles from assistant to coordinator to executive director.

In each movement location I felt inspired by how people can come together for something greater than ourselves, *and* I felt a yearning for more.

Throughout this path of my jobs, I was always facilitating, within and beyond the organizations I served. At its most fundamental, facilitation is the art of making things easy, making it easier for humans to work together and get things done.

"There is a difference between 'simple' and 'easy.' Simple as in the 'relatively simple interactions' of emergence, easy as in 'facilitation is the art of making things easy.' I don't think they are the same, and I have a hunch the difference might be important and that maybe it should be explicit. Simple means that it boils down to relationships between individual people, objects, beings, truths. Ease has more to do with the amount of friction (or understanding) between the peopleobjectsbeingstruths. And part of what can clear a path to making things easier is to name the simple interactions at play in a complex system."
—Rachel Plattus

I think facilitation is rooted in a certain grand love for life. I've recently realized that I come from a family of facilitators, though everyone wouldn't describe themselves that way.

As I mentioned, my parents are an interracial couple who fell in love in the deep South in the mid-seventies. I am sure I will write their love story one day, but for the purpose of this book it's mostly important to know that both of them had to be able to see something *impossible* (based on the families and society they'd been born into) as not only a *possible* way forward, but as the best way forward.

In their family, work, and community roles over the years, both my parents have shown a natural capacity for leading groups, organizing tasks, making things easier for those around them. They have navigated a wide range of political and economic difference in our extended family.

I have two sisters, both of whom I look to as teachers and confidantes. We are each very different, and yet we all seem to be oriented towards facilitation, consensus, and mediation work.

In our lifetimes, being multiracial has become more common, but navigating other peoples' regressive, fearful, or exoticizing ideas about our identities is one of the ways each member of my immediate family grew this skill set of being able to see what's between, what connects the things that seem separate, the ever-present whole.

I also have to speak here of my evangelical maternal grandfather, Fred Mathis, who facilitated many conversations about Jesus, morality, spirit, faith, and love in his lifetime. Every single time I was in his presence, I was amazed at how quickly we were in a conversation of his choosing, where he was really listening to my child-thoughts about god and love and duty, where I felt I could be honest, even with my doubts, even with my heart. We often differed in opinion, which, with him, felt safe and even invited in a way that it wasn't and hasn't been with most other southern white people. We would talk, and then he would get me on a horse and take me to the woods, asking me intermittently if I understood how powerful the horse was, how beautiful the land was. Though he was not a fan of my queer sexuality—the only letter I have from him includes scripture and sadness in response to my somewhat impetuous (but accurate) assertion that "I like to sleep with everybody!"—he let me come back to his table and before he left this plane we created room to recognize each other's humanity and spirituality. I came to understand his fears were rooted in love for me and concern for my eternal soul. He came to understand I was going to find my own way, and that I loved him and was living a life he couldn't imagine. I learned from him the art of conversation, faith, and silence.

My paternal grandmother, Elouise Brown, died when I was nine. One of my clearest secret memories is that I saw her, impossibly, on a playground, shortly before I learned of her death. As I get older, I think part of her came to me to be carried for a while; I have felt her with me so closely. Most of her lessons have been passed down to me through stories about her, patched together with sparse deep memories of her hands in my hair: her door was always open, there was something to eat, the neighborhood kids knew they could come open her deep freezer for a popsicle. She had seven children of her own. From her I learned that food is an important foundation for community, and that love isn't always a doorway to forever...sometimes it is a door to another love. Always it is an emergent process.

Among other things, love is an energy of possibility: the possibility of wholeness, in a Platonic understanding. I come from a lineage of brave and radical love, and I don't think it is an accident that love has been such an overt and active force in my life and that I have come to the conclusion that there is a science of love, a science of transformation and acceptance and gratitude that can help us to be better humans. So I will draw on that love experience as data as much as any other data presented in this book.

Below are some of the other aspects of who I am in this lineage, and what shapes the content gathered here.

Pleasure Activist

I picked up this term from harm reductionist[26] Keith Cylar, who I met only briefly before he passed on April 5, 2004 after twenty years of living with HIV. Initially pleasure activism was about claiming our right to experience pleasure, to be safe and respected in the pleasures we choose.

It has expanded for me over the years as I have come to believe that facts, guilt, and shame are limited motivations for creating change, even though those are the primary forces we use in our organizing work. I suspect that to really transform our society, we will need to make justice one of the most pleasurable experiences we can have.[27]

We also have to stop demonizing pleasure. We try to leverage control over the natural world by making our emotions and sensations less reliable than our thoughts, and then burn at the stake anyone who stays attuned to the ways and power of pleasure in the natural world. It's counter productive.

Audre Lorde's essay *The Uses of the Erotic* is foundational writing on the radical act of tuning into pleasure and not settling for less than the erotic sense of wholeness and rightness in one's life. She is my ancestor in the lineage of this particular work and many others.

I will speak many times of BOLD, the leadership development for Black organizers that is one of my favorite political homes. What we do there is turn and face reality, engage in deep relationship, and love up on each other. It is an organizing space that is also a maroon space, and it is

---

26 Harm Reduction is an approach to policy and care that reduces the harm that comes from drugs, alcohol, sex and sex work, and other legal and illegal human behaviors. For a good introduction, visit http://harmreduction.org/about-us/principles-of-harm-reduction/

27 DJ scholar Lynnée Denise, a core relationship and learning ground in my life, speaks of this as "misery resistance." She notices the practices, particularly in Black communities, of dancing, singing, and loving as forms of resisting and releasing oppression from the collective Black body.

always a pleasure to enter.[28] Every member of BOLD is a teacher of mine.

What we pay attention to grows—this is a hard world, but it is also a world full of love and pleasure. I am of that, attending to and growing that. That, to me, is pleasure activism. I am pretty certain that the next book I write will be on pleasure activism.

Healer/Doula

We all have the capacity to heal each other—healer is a possibility in each of us.

In my experience, healing happens when a place of trauma or pain is given full attention, really listened to. Healing is the resilience instinct of our bodies, a skill we unlearn as we are taught to pay for and rely on data and medicine outside of our own awareness to be well. I have been discovering, or surrendering, to my gifts as a healer. There is a way I can open up my presence, voice, and touch to an energy greater than what my body or life has given me. Then truth, comfort, ease, release, and other healing experiences can flow through, wholeness and acceptance of what is can be felt. I have studied reiki, massage, somatic bodywork, voice healing, tarot, and witchcraft as I have felt my healer capacity emerge.

I place doula here because the work feels the same—a doula, or birth supporter, is specifically a person who supports a pregnant person before, during, and after childbirth. The role was traditionally held by women in the family or community, often working with a midwife or doctor in the process. Childbirth these days is one of the clearest examples

---

28 "People are constantly creating what we call 'maroon spaces'—free communities, free platforms for thought and expression. I think that that's just in the DNA of Black Atlantic culture…. There's always the imperative towards the emancipated space."—Greg Tate, from an interview with Giovanni Russonello, April 30, 2015, http://www.capitalbop.com/greg-tate-on-burnt-sugar-afrofuturism-and-the-maroon-spaces-that-music-allows/.

of humans working against nature—hence the norms of sterile medicated hospital births with a drastic increase in scheduled inductions and unnecessary C-sections.

I learned of these trends away from natural birth when my sister Autumn started having her babies, and she taught me a ton with her choices. I had been asked several times to be a doula and kept saying no, because BLOOD! and the proximity of the words "vagina" and "tear" didn't feel like it was going to work for me.

Then a woman was attacked with a hammer behind my apartment while I was living in Oakland and I was the first to find her and comfort her as she bled and struggled to stay conscious. I saw her strength and aliveness and held it with her until the ambulance came. When she came to thank me a week later we spoke of how we had created a future for her together.

After that experience, and inspired by Autumn, I said yes the next time I was asked to become a doula, learning as an apprentice to Cynthia Jackson in Detroit.[29] Eventually I got to be present for the birth of Autumn's third child, and be part of her support during the miscarriage of her fourth child. Life and death are transitions that want to be held gently.

I have now been a doula and birth supporter for several births. The final read through of this book was actually delayed because a dear friend brought a perfect little one into the world and I was her doula and could not look away from the first weeks of that precious being's life.

Beyond birth, I have found doula to be a role that applies to many aspects of life. Birthwork teaches us to engage tension, but not to indulge drama. It is another form of facilitation, making the miraculous experience of birth as easy as

---

29   Cynthia Jackson grew up in a home of natural birth and many siblings, and has been working as a doula as long as she can remember. She is now working as a home birth midwife and doula in Detroit. More information about her work can be found at http://www.sacredrosebirthingservices.com/.

possible, intervening with any systems that make the process harder, helping the family attend to each other and listen to what the body is saying, staying focused on the possibility and wisdom of the body. Standing or sitting with someone as they realize, remember their own wholeness—that is the work of the healer and the doula.

My healing work is just pushing back the external world, making more space for people to feel themselves. Detroit musician/spiritual teacher/friend Sterling Toles told me he considers himself a "dressing room where people can try on their most authentic selves," and this has been a guiding visual for me when I am engaged in my healing work. As he said in the opening of the 2016 Allied Media Conference, "It's ok to feel beautiful in the process of creating justice."

Writer/Artist

My mom says writing came first, and it certainly has been the most consistent kind of work I have done in my life, writing, creating, drawing, singing. I am better at some forms of creating than others, but I enjoy all of it. And I have to write, in some form, every day. It's how I understand the world.

Toni Cade Bambara, a Black feminist writer-organizer who left lots of wisdom for us, said two things that I turn to when I start to wonder if art is enough of a contribution. On one hand, as I referenced earlier, she said "The role of the artist is to make the revolution irresistible."[30] On the other hand, she said that "Writing is one of the ways I participate in transformation." From this wisdom combination, I see that I am charged to write about the revolutions I long for, and that any writing I do, even if it isn't explicitly political, is still a transformative act. I apply this to my songs, my self-portraits, my poems—understanding that when a Black, queer, thick artist woman intentionally takes up space, it creates a new world.

---

30   Interview by Kay Bonetti, 1982.

Independent Science/Visionary Fiction Scholar

I read sci fi and visionary fiction as political, sacred, and philosophical text, and I engage with others who read it that way. I spent the first part of my life learning what history's victors wanted to tell me to believe about the past, including the simple assumption that it was the past. I see massive patterns of violence and inequality in history, which perpetuate in the daily news. Science fiction, particularly visionary fiction, is where I go when I need the medicine of possibility applied to the trauma of human behavior. While I have done deep dives in the work of Samuel Delaney, Ursula Le Guin, and others, I started this scholarship in earnest with Octavia. She presented perspectives on the future that were terrifying and compelling, and she took my breath away with her ideas for how to navigate change.

She said:

> *all that you touch*
> *you change*
> *all that you change*
> *changes you*
> *the only lasting truth*
> *is change*
> *god is change*[31]

If we accept the scientific and science fictional premise that change is a constant condition of this universe, then it becomes important that we learn to be in right relationship with change.

After much deliberation I have opted not to include a bunch of Butler analysis and spoilers in this book—her work is incredibly strong and clear. If you haven't read it, feel free to put this book down and go read everything she wrote[32] and

---

31　Butler, *Parable of the Sower*.

32　Including *Survivor*, which was published by Doubleday in 1978 but never reprinted because Octavia didn't like it, calling it her "*Star Trek* novel." I think it is a useful read to see her growth and idea formation.

then pick this back up. Warning: I reference her constantly and casually in these pages, as if you have also read the work and know what I am talking about.

That's true of almost everyone I reference—this book is not about analyzing other people's books or work. If you want more, go read the people and books I reference, and then consume the works they reference. I want to move forward from where others ended, or at least from the point of impact between their work and my own.

So Wheatley, Boggs, Butler, my family, my passions—all of these are teachers of emergence for me.

I have also been impressed and developed by the speeches of biomimicry teacher Janine Benyus, the mycelium/mushroom scholar Paul Stametz, the organizing model of Ella Baker, the Toltec worldview presented in *The Four Agreements* by Don Miguel Ruiz, and the *Tao Te Ching* by Lao Tzu (particularly the interpretations of Stephen Mitchell and Le Guin).

I have learned that feeling matters, that feeling is an important and legitimate way of knowing. This learning has come most formally through Somatics (particularly the social justice and somatics blend found in generative somatics, through the work of Staci Haines, Spenta Kandawalla, Liu Hoi-man, Lisa Thomas Adeyemo, Chris Lymbertos, Vassilissa Johri, and Richard Strozzi-Heckler), and Robert Gass's work on the art of transformation now developing and evolving into emergent strategies at the Social Transformation Project under the leadership of Jodie Tonita, Eugene Kim, Idelisse Malave, and others.

And *Star Wars* (the force); William Gibson (Idoru); China Mieville (dream shit); Nalo Hopkinson (sensual breathtaking magic); the Zapatistas (many worlds exist); the Black Panthers (meet the biological needs of a community as a mode of organizing); Black feminist artists Audre Lorde, June Jordan, Lucille Clifton, and Toni Cade Bambara (create as a form of revolution); Gloria Anzaldúa; and many more.

Early on in my exploration of this kind of work, Marianne Manilov and Alissa Hauser, network cultivators, invited me to hold a year of community practice with the Engage Network. They and the participants in that year-long journey were also teachers—Anasa Troutman, Kerri Kelly, Jenny Lee, Jodie Tonita, Jane Sung E Bai, Gibran Rivera, Mike Norman, Jidan Koon, and Navina Khanna, thank you.

I also held a transformative phone-based community of practice for a year after a Creative Change gathering in Utah. It had some very vulnerable and beautiful emergent elements to it that taught me about curating soil that is fertile for relationship building.

And then there are all the other incredible people whose voices are woven throughout this book and online appendix. They each taught me something about emergent strategy. And there are many more teachers whose voices are not in this book.

I think that is the best I can do on explicit lineage—feel free to remind me of anything I missed. Basically, I see emergence everywhere and I feel positively obsessed with the possibilities of being awake to it.

"Without positive obsession, there is nothing at all."
—Octavia Butler[33]

---

33   Butler, *Parable of the Sower*.

PRINCIPLES OF EMERGENT STRATEGY

In the study and practice of emergent strategy, there are core principles that have emerged and that guide me in learning and using this idea and method in the world. I gather them here with the expectation that they will grow.

Small is good, small is all. (The large is a reflection of the small.)

Change is constant. (Be like water).[1]

There is always enough time for the right work.

There is a conversation in the room that only these people at this moment can have.[2] Find it.

Never a failure, always a lesson.[3]

---

1   "You must be shapeless, formless, like water. When you pour water in a cup, it becomes the cup. When you pour water in a bottle, it becomes the bottle. When you pour water in a teapot, it becomes the teapot. Water can drip and it can crash. Become like water my friend," Bruce Lee, *Bruce Lee: A Warrior's Journey* (Warner Home Video, 2000).

2   Idea articulated by Taj James in the cofacilitation of environmental justice resource redistribution initiative Building Equity and Alignment's inaugural meeting in 2013.

3   Rihanna has this concept tattooed on her chest.

Trust the People. (If you trust the people, they become trustworthy).[4]

Move at the speed of trust.[5] Focus on critical connections more than critical mass—build the resilience by building the relationships.

Less prep, more presence.

What you pay attention to grows.

---

4   This is an inversion of the quote "If you don't trust the people, they become untrustworthy," from Stephen Mitchell's translation, Lao Tzu, *Tao Te Ching* (New York: HarperCollins, 1988).

5   This is communications strategist Mervyn Marcano's remix of Stephen Covey's "speed of trust" concept.

ELEMENTS OF
EMERGENT STRATEGY

In both workshops and in writing this book, I've noticed that it's pretty impossible to completely separate any one of the elements of emergent strategy from the others.

Or rather, at the same time, each of these elements is distinct and is totally connected to every other element. When I speak about them, they shift in my mouth. In writing this book, seven elements became six, and they rearranged themselves several times to land in this order. It is not random, but it is not right either—it's just where things landed.

I have seen other people learning about emergence and applying it to human systems and social justice systems in the world as well, and they have made good sense to me.

For example, Complex Movements is a Detroit-based artist collective supporting the transformation of communities by exploring the connections of complex science and social justice movements through multimedia interactive performance work. The Complex Movements crew uses an emblem system with ferns, ants, wavicles, mycelium, and more to engage communities in thinking about the formations and movements of the future.

The particular organization of elements I present here is a snapshot of a theory in perpetual motion. This is the current configuration, which gives me the most space to reflect on my experiences in social justice movements, to invite others into conversation about how we work, and to articulate my longing for something different. One of the ways I was able to identify these was by formulating my critique of the ways that social justice movements have felt, and where my longing for something else was strongest.

Grace often said that every crisis is an opportunity, which is amazing theoretically, and requires great emotional fortitude in practice, as well as the maturity to understand that the negative realization of that theory is "disaster capitalism."[1]

---

1   Naomi Klein, *The Shock Doctrine: The Rise of Disaster Capitalism* (New York: Picador, 2008).

Complex Movements is also studying the relationship between emergence and movements for social justice. Their emblem system is a gorgeous way of learning properties of nature we can apply to our work.

Mycelium *is the part of the fungus that grows underground in thread-like formations. It connects roots to one another and breaks down plant material to create healthier ecosystems. Mycelium is the largest organism on earth. Interconnectedness. Remediation. Detoxification.*

Ants. *Ant societies function through individual ants acting collectively in accord with simple, local information to carry on all of their survival activities. Every ant relies on the work of others in producing their own work. Cooperative work. Collective Sustainability.*

Ferns *are a form of fractal. A fractal is an object or quantity that displays self similarity, which means it looks roughly the same at any scale. Small-scale solutions impact the whole system. Use similar principles to build at all scales.*

The **Wavicle***, or wave-particle duality, suggests that all objects exhibit both wave and partical properties. Between observations as it evolves on its own, it behaves like a wave; distributed across space, exploring different intermixing paths to all possible destinations. However, when its location or speed is measured, it appears definite and concrete, like a particle. Its wave nature gives this measurement a curious property: the more certain we are about either speed or position, the more uncertain we become about the other. Uncertainty/doubt. Valuing both process and outcome.*

Starlings. *The synchronized movement patterns of a starling flock is also known as a murmuration. Guided by simple rules, starling murmurations can react to their environment as a group without a central leader orchestrating their choices; in any instant, any part of the flock can transform the movement of the whole flock. Collective leadership/ partnership. Adaptability.*

Dandelions. *The dandelion flower head can change into a white, globular seed head overnight. Each seed has a tiny parachute that allows it to spread far and wide in the wind. The entire plant has medicinal properties. Dandelions are often mistakenly identified as weeds, aggressively removed, but are hard to uproot; the top is pulled but the long taproot remains. Resilience. Resistance. Regeneration. Decentralization.*

Sitting with the questions of how I could transform some of the heartbreak I have experienced in nonprofit work into lessons that could offer other paths forward, I found that part of the opportunity was to pay deeper attention to how the natural world has solved these same problems. I do believe that what we pay attention to grows, so I wanted to stop growing the crises, the critique. The elements in this book are a way to shift my attention to the positive, to what I want to grow.

I like the word *biomimicry*, and I love knowing that the practices of mimicking the natural world have been happening since humans came into existence. This is actually an ancient practice, a recovery rather than a discovery.

"Biomimicry is basically taking a design challenge and then finding an ecosystem that has already

solved that challenge, and literally trying to emu-
late what you learn. There are three types of biomimicry—one is copying form and shape, another
is copying a process, like photosynthesis in a leaf,
and the third is mimicking at an ecosystem's level,
like building a nature-inspired city."
—Janine Benyus

The elements I explore reference aspects of the natural
world operating at each of these levels, though the bulk of
examples aim at the systems and processes.

For each of these elements, we spiral from the simple
understanding to the more complex ways of thinking about
applying the element to our movement work. I define what
the element is according to a dictionary, point out some of
the places we see this element in nature, then offer up writing
I've done on the element, moving from the personal through
organizational to movement or collective levels. Towards
the end is a brief assessment tool you can use to reflect on
how much emergent strategy is showing up in your life and
work. Then I share some of the emergent strategy practices
and tools I have worked with to create tangible differences in
movement work.

I'll add this because of some of the doubt I've seen people
experience when approaching these concepts—some people
are more comfortable with emergent strategy than others, but
I don't think this has to do with personality or intelligence.
We are already emergent beings, just by our very existence.
But we've been tricked away from it.

Nature vs. nurture is part of this—and then there is what
I think of as anti-nurturing—the ways we in a western/US
context are socialized to work against respecting the emergent processes of the world and each other:

- We learn to disrespect Indigenous and direct
  ties to land.

- We learn to be quiet, polite, indirect, and submissive, not to disturb the status quo.
- We learn facts out of context of application in school. How will this history, science, math show up in our lives, in the work of growing community and home?
- We learn that tests and deadlines are the reasons to take action. This puts those with good short-term memories and a positive response to pressure in leadership positions, leading to urgency-based thinking, regardless of the circumstance.
- We learn to compete with each other in a scarcity-based economy that denies and destroys the abundant world we actually live in.
- We learn to deny our longings and our skills, and to do work that occupies our hours without inspiring our greatness.
- We learn to manipulate each other and sell things to each other, rather than learning to collaborate and evolve together.
- We learn that the natural world is to be manicured, controlled, or pillaged to support our consumerist lives. Even the natural lives of our bodies get medicated, pathologized, shaved or improved upon with cosmetic adjustments.
- We learn that factors beyond our control determine the quality of our lives—something as random as which skin, gender, sexuality, ability, nation, or belief system we are born into sets a path for survival and quality of life.
- In the United States specifically, though I see this most places I travel, we learn that we only have value if we can produce—only then do we earn food, home, health care, education.
- Similarly, we learn our organizations are only as successful as our fundraising results, whether the community impact is powerful or not.

- We learn as children to swallow our tears and any other inconvenient emotions, and as adults that translates into working through red flags, value differences, pain, and exhaustion.
- We learn to bond through gossip, venting, and destroying, rather than cultivating solutions together.
- Perhaps the most egregious thing we are taught is that we should just be really good at what's already possible, to leave the impossible alone.

Lots of people and organizations have been and are critical of these ways we socialize each other, and have offered solutions—I think here of Harriet Tubman, Ella Baker, Frantz Fanon, Karl Marx, Augusto Boal, Malcolm X, the Zapatistas, and others throughout history who I believe have felt the thrum of emergence in their systems and moved what was possible in their lifetimes such that their impacts reverberate in my life and the work of my generation.

We are still mostly misdirected, turned away from the wisdom that is our inheritance. Joanna Macy speaks of the "great turning," a collective awakening and shifting direction, away from the wanton destruction of this planet and each other, away from those practices of separation and competition listed above, towards life and abundance.[2] I like this visual of turning and evolving, as opposed to destroying the systems in place now.

When Wheatley visited Detroit on a learning journey, she said systems built on greed eventually collapse on themselves, topple under their own top-heavy weight.

Matter doesn't disappear, it transforms. Energy is the same way. The Earth is layer upon layer of all that has existed, remembered by the dirt. It is time to turn capitalism into a fossil, time to turn the soil, turn to the horizon together.

---

2   To learn more about Joanna Macy's work, I recommend visiting her website, http://www.joannamacy.net/thegreatturning.html.

If, as you are engaging these elements, a clearer framework appears, or an additional piece, that's good news. Let's all be conduits of the wisdom of this planet. I think any efforts to engage the emergent brilliance of our world will help with this turning, will help with liberating humanity from its current role as a virus Earth should shake off.

So, without further ado, the elements:

Element	Nature of Element
Fractal	The Relationship Between Small and Large
Adaptative	How We Change
Interdependence and Decentralization	Who We Are and How We Share
Non-linear and Iterative	The Pace and Pathways of Change
Resilience and Transformative Justice	How We Recover and Transform
Creating More Possibilities	How We Move Towards Life

FRACTALS:

the relationship between small and large

A **fractal** is a never-ending pattern. Fractals are infinitely complex patterns that are self-similar across different scales. They are created by repeating a simple process over and over in an ongoing feedback loop.

grounding in nature

"The micro reflects the macro and vice versa—Fibonacci patterns show up from space to cauliflower. The tiniest most mundane act reflects the biggest creations we can imagine."
—Kat Aaron

Tune in to the prevalence of spiral in the universe—the shape in the prints of our fingertips echoes into geological patterns, all the way to the shape of galaxies. Then notice that the planet is full of these fractals—cauliflower, yes, and broccoli, ferns, deltas, veins through our bodies, tributaries, etc.—all of these are

> echoes of themselves at the smallest and
> largest scales. Dandelions contain an entire
> community in each spore that gets blown on
> children's breath.

How we are at the small scale is how we are at the large
scale. The patterns of the universe repeat at scale. There is a
structural echo that suggests two things: one, that there are
shapes and patterns fundamental to our universe, and two,
that what we practice at a small scale can reverberate to the
largest scale.

I first became aware of fractals in 2004 when I was doing electoral organizing, though I didn't have the word for it.
We were trying to impact the federal election, to get George
W. Bush out of office. And what I saw clearly was that, at a
local level, we—Americans—don't know how to do democ-
racy. We don't know how to make decisions together, how
to create generative compromises, how to advance policies
that center justice. Most of our movements are reduced to
advancing false solutions, things we can get corporate or gov-
ernmental agreement on, which don't actually get us where
we need to be. It was and is devastatingly clear to me that until we have some sense of how to live our solutions locally, we
won't be successful at implementing a just governance system
regionally, nationally, or globally.

This awareness led me to look at organizations more
critically. So many of our organizations working for social
change are structured in ways that reflect the status quo.
We have singular charismatic leaders, top down structures,
money-driven programs, destructive methods of engaging
conflict, unsustainable work cultures, and little to no impact on the issues at hand. This makes sense; it's the water
we're swimming in. But it creates patterns. Some of the
patterns I've seen that start small and then become movement wide are:

- Burn out. Overwork, underpay, unrealistic expectations.
- Organizational and movement splitting.
- Personal drama disrupting movements.
- Mission drift, specifically in the direction of money.
- Stagnation—an inability to make decisions.

These patterns emerge at the local, regional, state, national, and global level—basically wherever two or more social change agents are gathered. There's so much awareness around it, and some beautiful work happening to shift organizational cultures. And this may be the most important element to understand—that *what we practice at the small scale sets the patterns for the whole system.*

Grace articulated it in what might be the most-used quote of my life: "*Transform yourself to transform the world.*" This doesn't mean to get lost in the self, but rather to see our own lives and work and relationships as a front line, a first place we can practice justice, liberation, and alignment with each other and the planet.

In my own life this understanding has created major shifts. Once upon a time I was a burnt out executive director, tied to my technology and my sense of my own importance. When I was with friends, family, lovers, I was still working. I thought I was awesome at multitasking. I would say urgency, obligation, and specialness were the driving forces in my life. I was using food, drink, sex, and work to numb my way through life. My work was reactive; there was often a sense of time scarcity and sprinting, of hopelessness, of not being appreciated, feeling no trust, of working with a confused vision.

My family intervened in a variety of ways, primarily by noticing aloud how little they felt me. I had gotten this feedback from others as well, that when I wasn't "on" it was hard to *feel* me. When I was "on" I could fill a room.

My coworkers also let me know how frustrating it was to work with me when I was so clearly unhappy.

In 2012 I took a sabbatical, and I realized that I wasn't upholding my end of the sacred bargain: My life is a miracle that cannot be recreated. I can never get these hours, weeks, years back. In a fractal conception, I am a cell-sized unit of the human organism, and I have to use my life to leverage a shift in the system by *how* I am, as much as with the things I do. This means actually being in my life, and it means bringing my values into my daily decision making. Each day should be lived on purpose.

This has meant increasing my intentionality about being with others. Adapting to the changes of life, yes, but with a clear and transparent intention to keep deepening with my loved ones and transforming together.

I struggle with putting the phone/devices down like most people in my generation or younger, but I am learning to savor the quality of time spent without them, in real life with other people, with my writing, being present. Or using the Internet and cellular data to build trust and connection, rather than to echo chamber deconstruction and destruction.

It has meant getting in touch with my body and feelings in real time, and learning to express them. I am learning to engage in generative conflict, to say no, to feel my limits, taking time to feel my heartache when it comes—from living in America, from interpersonal trauma or grief, from movement losses.

It has meant learning to work collaboratively, which goes against my inner "specialness." I am socialized to seek achievement alone, to try to have the best idea and forward it through the masses. But that leads to loneliness and, I suspect, extinction. If we are all trying to win, no one really ever wins.

I am beginning to revel in the increased capacity that comes from working with and trusting others. I sleep, I center, I travel, I share. I have offered more room in my life to love, family, creating. Each day I feel more authentic, and more capable. I don't experience failure much these days; I experience growth.

I have increased my practices of collaboration and storytelling as ways to share analysis, engaging and facilitating deep small transformations that pick up and echo each other towards a tipping point, organizing based in love and care rather than burnout and competition.

At a collective level, this is the invitation to practice the world we wish to see in the current landscape. Yes, resist the onslaught of oppression, but measure our success not just by what we stop, but by how many of us feel, and can say:

> I am living a life I don't regret
> A life that will resonate with my ancestors,[1]
> and with as many generations forward as I can
>   imagine.
> I am attending to the crises of my time with
>   my best self,
> I am of communities that are doing our collec-
>   tive best
> to honor our ancestors and all humans to
>   come.

It's lifework, with benefits. I regularly check in with my vision for our collective future and make adjustments on how I am living, what I am practicing, to be aligned with that future, to make it more possible.

That's a little testifying and spell casting on how fractal work feels on a personal level. Here are two explorations of it in organizing work—couching fractals in the idea of what movements need today followed by a piece about how

---

1   Mary Hooks of Southerners on New Ground and #blacklivesmatter Atlanta offers a mandate for Black people that moves me as I build towards this life of no regrets: "To avenge the suffering of my ancestors, to earn the respect of future generations, and to be transformed in the service of the work." I have been using this mandate in my work for Black liberation (http://southernersonnewground.org/2016/07/themandate/).

Ruckus, a small and mighty organization, shifted its practices to be aligned with its values.

"The only way to deal with an unfree world is to become so absolutely free that your very existence is an act of rebellion."
—Albert Camus

Notes from "Intersecting Worlds: The One We've Got, The One We're Building, The Ones We Imagine"[2]

My vision is changing our *how*, more than seeing clearly our *what*. I see a how where we are all much more comfortable with change, and with our personal power to change conditions.

Some people are comfortable believing—in heaven, in socialism, in someone else's thinking. That's never quite worked for me. I learn experientially. I am so far only convinced that change is divine and constant.

Octavia Butler said, "Belief initiates and guides action—Or it does nothing."[3] In her twelve novels and her short stories, she created case studies that teach how to lead inside of change, shaping change. I've been calling what I learn from her work emergent strategy. Based in the science of emergence, it's relational, adaptive, fractal, interdependent, decentralized, transformative. I'm applying it in facilitation and organizational development work.

---

2   This section is based on notes I wrote before a keynote panel at the New Economy Coalition's CommonBound conference in June 2014. My fellow panelists were Gar Alperovitz and Gopal Dayaneni, and we were facilitated by Rachel Plattus. You can see the whole discussion at https://www.youtube.com/watch?v=n0eI9jJRGyk.

3   Butler, *Parable of the Sower*.

It unleashes more of the power of each person.

Because some are comfortable deferring the work of vision to others—or being the visionary talkers (I am guilty of being a visionary talker for years! Forgive me.[4]). I think, and have been gathering proof in sci fi writing workshops with organizers and activists, that we each have important pieces of the whole, so I concentrate my work on the generation of vision, the strengthening of the muscle of looking forward together.

One major emerging lesson: We have to create futures in which everyone doesn't have to be the same kind of person. That's the problem with most utopias for me: they are presented as mono value, a new greener more local monoculture where everyone gardens and plays the lute and no one travels... And I don't want to go there![5]

Compelling futures have to have more justice, yes; and right relationship to planet, yes; but also must allow for our growth and innovation. I want an interdependence of lots of kinds of people with lots of belief systems, *and* continued evolution.

Right now we don't know what's right so much as we know what's wrong, and what we've tried. And based on how constantly surprised I still am by life every day, I suspect that will likely continue to be the case, and hopefully, perpetually resolving these major issues continues to be interesting. My mentor Grace Lee Boggs is still curious on the eve of her ninety-ninth birthday, so I'm hopeful.

Nothing that has existed so far was the right way for everyone, but there are pieces out there we can begin to imagine together. This is why Gar Alperovitz's writing speaks to me— what's between capitalism and socialism?[6] Because whatever

---

4   See "Confessions of a Charismatic Leader" later in this book.

5   Paraphrasing Liz Lemon, *30 Rock* (NBC, 2011).

6   To read more about Gar Alperovitz's exploration of the space between capitalism and socialism, visit http://garalperovitz.com/ ifyoudontlike/.

we build will stand on the foundations of those economic experiments. This is why Gopal Dayaneni's work appeals to me—what are the strategies we need to learn, with appropriate fear and wonder, to move our movements into right relationship with the planet?[7] Let's learn.

I want a future where we are curious, interested, visionary, adaptive.

The community in Detroit, to which I am still a newcomer, has been in transition for decades. We are learning about tolerating, even recently—a few years ago foundations were investing in us, now they aren't as much, and it has impact. Generally we have to let go of the success that we feel, as individuals and organizations, when capitalism works for us.

Gopal convinced me years ago that we need to have a level of dystopian consideration. Certain climate realities are no longer wild imaginings, they are happening, and they are coming. (*Game of Thrones* watchers? Winter is here, and it's balmy.) Octavia Butler appeals to me because she wanted to prepare us for inevitable consequences of human behavior.

That is the context in which I enter this conversation. I don't have answers, but I am sitting with these questions:

Change is coming—what do we need to imagine as we prepare for it?

What is compelling about surviving climate change?

What is a just transition economy?[8] What is an economy for the phase of transition from this way of relating to Earth and resources, to the way we might relate on a watered Earth, or a frozen Earth?

---

7   To read more about Gopal Dayaneni's work with the other brilliant members of the Movement Generation team, visit http://movement generation.org/.

8   Movement Generation taught me that *economy* simply means the management of home, of the resources of home. A functional economy is a universal concern.

How do we prepare not just for suffering, but for sharing and innovation?

How do we resource the local and still honor our nomadic tendency, our natural migration patterns (which we deny by trying to stay in only one place), our global interconnectedness?

How do we prepare the children in our lives to be visionary, and to love nature even when the changes are frightening and incomprehensible? To be abundant when what we consider valuable is shifting from gold to collard greens?

How do we articulate a compelling economic vision to sustain us through the unimaginable, to unite us as things fall apart?

How do we experience our beauty and humanity in every condition?

These are the questions that sustain my work. I believe all of you hold answers.

We hone our skills of naming and analyzing the crises. I learned in school how to *de*construct—but how do we move beyond our beautiful deconstruction? Who teaches us to reconstruct?

How do we cultivate the muscle of radical imagination needed to dream together beyond fear? Showing Black and white people sitting at a lunch counter together was science fiction.

We need to move from competitive ideation, trying to push our individual ideas, to collective ideation, collaborative ideation. It isn't about having the number one best idea, but having ideas that come from, and work for, more people.

When we speak of systemic change, we need to be fractal. Fractals—a way to speak of the patterns we see—move from the micro to macro level. The same spirals on sea shells can be found in the shape of galaxies. We must create patterns that cycle upwards. We are microsystems. (We each hold contradictions—my shellac nails vs. my desire that no one do the toxic work of nail painting, my family travel vs. my desire not to use fossil fuels, etc.). Our friendships and relationships are systems. Our communities are systems. Let us practice upwards.

And then—what happens when we succeed? New problems? Detroit filmmaker Oya Amakisi once shared with me the words of General Baker, a Detroit labor organizer and leader, who said, "You keep asking how do we get the people here? I say, what will we do when they get here?"

Maya Angelou's "On the Pulse of Morning" feels incredibly relevant here today:

> Each new hour holds new chances
> For new beginnings.
> Do not be wedded forever
> To fear, yoked eternally
> To brutishness.
>
> The horizon leans forward,
> Offering you space to place new steps of
>   change[9].

Transforming Ruckus: Actions Speak Louder[10]

I am going to tell you a story about one organization's transformation from good intentions to good practice. The setting is the US social and environmental justice movement.

I was the executive director of The Ruckus Society for four and a half years, starting in 2006. Ruckus has historically been the kind of organization that wouldn't be described as feminist. Founded in 1996 on the model of Greenpeace action camps—get a hundred activists in the woods and show

---

9   Maya Angelou, *On the Pulse of Morning: The Inaugural Poem* (New York: Random House, 1993).

10   This was first published in *The Scholar and Feminist Online* Issue 8.3 (Summer 2010), http://sfonline.barnard.edu/polyphonic/brown_01 .htm.

them how to do non-violent civil disobedience in an effective way—Ruckus was rooted in a masculine action culture.

The best way I can explain this culture is penetrative. Rather than forming long-term partnerships with communities, Ruckus was in and out with mind-blowing, creative actions. This was in line with a model of action grounded in spectacle. The politics were radical and the actions historic, but there wasn't a sense of community ownership or engagement in the work—which meant that at a fundamental level the power dynamic wasn't changing. The communities still come to rely on someone else to change their situation.

Over years of amazing work, coupled with critiques about the approach, Ruckus went through what could perhaps be called labor pains to bring forth the model and structure we currently have—which includes a team of women, majority queer, at the staff level.

The frustrations folks had with Ruckus are very much the frustrations alive in our movements right now—we had a vision for the kind of world we wanted to see, but we weren't modeling that internally. We wanted strong local economies where communities felt responsible for their neighbors' well being, but Ruckus wasn't actually developing local direct action know-how.

Out of this moment in our history, a new program was born that transformed how we worked. It was called the Indigenous People's Power Project (IP3). The model was to build a body of Indigenous organizers who became action experts within their own communities. In the process of getting this project off the ground, Ruckus was challenged to grow into something we couldn't even have imagined.

We grew an immense amount.

I was honored to be a part of The Ruckus Society during this labor, this awakening, watching over a transition born of frustrations and critiques as well as an instinct that something better was possible.

We had to begin to practice deep, authentic collaboration. This meant a shift in how we move financial and human resources—there are enough people out there to support the movement(s) we need, but currently, organizations are pitted against each other to access money (less and less money), rather than creating and investing together to maximize a diversity of resources from money, to people, to spaces, to skills. Because we are not investing in a shared network of resources, it is easy to let structural and ideological particularities create deep splits throughout the non-profit sphere, rendering much of our work useless.

We couldn't continue that—we had to figure out what humility looked like on all sides in order to truly collaborate. This included making room on our board for folks in the IP3 program, shifting timelines to meet community needs, with folks on all sides being able to say we didn't know how to do this, and recommitting over and over, even when it seemed too hard to continue.

One thing that was highlighted for us was that, in the direct action realm, it's not unusual to see time and energy poured into actions that are more interesting/funny/creative than they are compelling to those we are trying to reach and/or life-changing to the communities taking action. To be clear, we are moving in a good direction in being funny and creative—we want to engage people—but our standards for communities taking the risks associated with direct action must be that the experience and the results are compelling, even life-changing.

We also learned a lot about breaking down the walls between different issue areas. Indigenous communities present a clear case of economic and environmental hardship, with residents highly recruited for the military, dealing with high levels of drug and alcohol dependence and a high rate of suicide. Through this lens it's easy to see that just coming with one piece of analysis wouldn't serve the big picture.

For successful movements, we need to develop strong, action-oriented communities that understand that their analysis and work cannot be limited to one struggle. Together, we must be advancing the frontline of our vision for a sustainable, just world. Our strategies must be more sophisti-cated and engaging than those of our opposition.

We learned that every member of the community holds pieces of the solution, even if we are all engaged in different layers of the work.

We learned to look for telltale signs that actions were community based. One indicator that things are off is when impacted communities and people of color get involved and they are put in the role of "performing the action," for ex-ample, having their photos taken, being spokespeople, or being asked to endorse or represent work they don't get to lead, etc., while most of the background organizing is still dominated by the folks who aren't impacted and won't be around long term to sustain the campaign or to be held accountable.

At its worst, this approach builds up hope and encourag-es local communities to take risks, and then abandons them with the results.

At its best, there is a moment of victory. But too often, in spite of their best intentions, those who aren't directly impact-ed only see the surface layer(s) of the impact, and thus come up with surface solutions that don't address the deep-seated multi-pronged need in the community.

We learned that in organizing and relationships, ac-countability is key for building a lasting base; when folks see change, they feel their own investment is worthwhile. We need actions that build our base, because we must reach a tipping point of folks who are on the side of justice before we reach the peak of what our planet can provide.

To be transparent, while Ruckus was in the midst of this transition, I didn't think of it as a transition from a patriar-chal organization to a feminist organization any more than I thought of it as a white organization becoming an organi-zation for people of color. I thought of our story as moving from a reactionary, surface-change direct-action organization to vision-based, systemic-change-oriented direct-action orga-nization. But all of the above happened.

Along the way we began to practice principles that felt necessary and powerful to articulate:

- Ruckus comes where we're called, respecting local work and building long-term relationships of support. We reach out to and build relationships with groups we respect, to lay the groundwork for being called to frontline work. We do not insert ourselves into people's political or community work.
- Ruckus supports action when the community most impacted by a political, social, economic, or environmental injustice is the leader of the strategy, vision, and action.
- Ruckus supports action that builds strength and holds space for a strong community vision.
- In a successful Ruckus action, the visions and solutions are deeper and more compelling than the injustice. (We are calling for a movement-wide shift away from action that isn't grounded in a vision of deep systemic change, as that ultimately is a misuse of our time and energy.)
- We submit that no social movement in history has successfully transformed its society without direct action, and we at Ruckus recognize our historical significance and the need for our work in the movement at this time. However, the actions that have had the most impact were uniquely suited to the time, place, and political conditions. We feel the movement has gotten stuck in a tactical rut and that it's time to leap out with actions that address our current political conditions directly.
- "Transform yourself to transform the world."—Grace Lee Boggs. We aim to be an organizational model of the change we call for in the world.

Now, in hindsight, I can see how we have transformed ourselves in a way that makes our work much more relevant as a living resistance to the dysfunctional social system in which we live. Within our small organization we have grown from a kickass, majority white, male-led environmental-issue-centered network into a kickass, female-led, multicultural, justice- AND environment-centered network.

We lovingly embrace those who brought the skills before us, and those to come, as part of the same fierce family of fearless activists with lifelong commitments to societal transformation. We are intentional about living our vision in terms of how we operate as a community in order to bring vision-based support to the movement we love. We opt for self-determination and sustainability in everything from our structure to our budgets to our programs.

We have learned that such a fundamental shift requires many small steps—having massive visions and making them attainable with specific goals that can be measured and felt both internally and by those who participate in the network and in our trainings.

We have also learned that we had to lay out our operating beliefs. Each person has a set of beliefs with which they move through the world. These are formed by their cultural, social, economic, and environmental (amongst others) experiences from birth, and they change as more experiences are added to the whole.

A group joins their beliefs together creating a set of named or unnamed ways in which they operate. We have made our beliefs very transparent at Ruckus. What we landed on was that, for the next period of history, we need to place an emphasis on:

- Impacted leadership (the leadership of communities directly impacted by economic and environmental injustice);
- Privileged support (the intentional support for impacted leadership from communities/people that can identify their privilege and want to see a rebalancing of power);

- Feminine leadership (not just women leaders, but leaders who shift our understanding of how power can be held).

These beliefs are partly grounded in the reality that leadership from these spheres is directly opposite to the leadership we've experienced for the last century and it's time for balance, and also because the most exciting organizing happening today is coming from communities directly impacted by oppressions and injustices.

As an organization, The Ruckus Society's operating principles include the "Jemez Principles" and the "Environmental Justice Principles." These principles mean we move towards our vision of sustainability and self-determination through organizing that values natural operating systems, understanding the power of uncovering the root causes of problems, and asking, "What are the root problems in my community, and what do deep, foundational, rooted solutions look like?" This is thinking from a place of healing, more than dominating others with our beliefs.

It is not enough to adhere to these values, however—we want to see our beliefs in practice.

Now, how does it feel?

Being a part of this team has been incredible. We have experienced what it's like to release any assumption that one person has all the skills needed to lead and support the work. That release—a huge relief to me personally—allowed us to begin to really weave together our strengths, rather than facing the limitations of relying on one leader to hold the vision, coordination, fundraising, and programmatic work of the group. It has allowed us to face our own personal limitations with transparency and curiosity, noting where we want to grow and not being afraid to ask for feedback.

On an average day, it feels like an extremely functional organization working for change. On the best days, it feels like the world we are trying to create, and it is marvelous.

INTENTIONAL
ADAPTATION:

how we change

---

adaptation: a change in a plant or animal that makes it better able to live in a particular place or situation; the process of changing to fit some purpose or situation: the process of adapting

intention: the thing that you plan to do or achieve: an aim or purpose

---

grounding in nature

"Starlings' murmuration consists of a flock moving in synch with one another, engaging in clear, consistent communication and exhibiting collective leadership and deep, deep trust. Every individual bird focuses attention on their seven closest neighbors and thus manage a larger flock cohesiveness and synchronicity (at times upwards of over a million birds)."
—Sierra Pickett

"Water is versatile. It can be big and powerful, it can quench thirst, it can be healing, it can drown us. It finds its own level, always. That is, water is always seeking balance and has a place it has to go. It can be scarce, it is necessary. We're utterly, devastatingly dependent on it. It's beautiful and tragic and it feeds us sometimes. When we hold water back we can create power but there is danger when we remove the dam unexpectedly. It's really flexible and adaptable. It takes the form of our containers. Bruce Lee says 'Be like water...' If we can understand fully the nature of water we can understand what we're doing here."

—Aisha Shillingford, *Intelligent Mischief*

"From water I have learned to move around and past fixed objects to reach my goal. From our winged kindred I have learned there are times to swarm and that such a swarm can take down even the largest and cockiest predator. But the most important lesson of all, for me, has been how history embeds in every living thing. The land speaks to me of a much longer time frame than the one my body understands. It reminds me that ours are generational fights that are passed down like legacy. The earth, in the way that it spins under our feet, changing while no one is looking, reminds me both that what we win today can be gone tomorrow, and what we lose today can be won tomorrow. The only constant is change. That is nature's greatest lesson to me—that change is inevitable, and time is unfathomable. It means I can keep

going, when all seems to fail and fall around
me. Nature is the source of my faith."
—Malkia Cyril

"Humankind is still evolving, in a process
which will never end. This evolution moves
on changing principles which are known only
to eternity. How can corrupt reasoning play
with such an essence?"
—Frank Herbert, *Dune*[1]

"A victim of God may,
Through learning adaptation,
Become a partner of God."
—Octavia Butler

Intentional adaptation is the heart of emergent strategy.
How we live and grow and stay purposeful in the face of
constant change actually does determine both the quality of
our lives, and the impact that we can have when we move
into action together.

Many of us respond to change with fear, or see it as a
crisis.[2] Some of us anticipate change with an almost titillating
sense of stress. We spend precious time thinking about what
has changed that we didn't choose or can't control, and/or
thinking ahead to future stress.

Often this is because we aren't clear or committed about
our dream destination, so instead of moving towards anything
in particular, we are in nonstop reaction. A first question to ask
ourselves is, how do we practice increasing our ease with what

---

1   If you have not read Frank Herbert's sci-fi classic *Dune*, put this book
     down and go read it.

2   "Fear is the mind-killer"—get this reference? You should if you ad-
     hered to the previous footnote. Just saying.

is? Change happens. Change is definitely going to happen, no matter what we plan or expect or hope for or set in place. We will adapt to that change, or we will become irrelevant.

But this element is not about pure adaptation, which has led to every functional and dysfunctional condition we know. I am talking about the combination of adaptation with intention, wherein the orientation and movement towards life, towards longing, is made graceful in the act of adaptation. This is the process of changing while staying in touch with our deeper purpose and longing.

In movement work, I have been facilitating groups to shift from a culture of strategic planning to one of strategic intentions—what are our intentions, informed by our vision? What do we need to be and do to bring our vision to pass? How do we bring those intentions to life throughout every change, in every aspect of our work?

This often results in groups centering work that doesn't depend on factors outside of their control (such as funders, or elections, which come and go and should be well used but not directive or debilitating). The clearer you are as a group about where you're going, the more you can relax into collaborative innovation around how to get there. You can relax into decentralization, and you want to.

If the vision is only clear to one person, that person ends up trying to drive everyone towards their vision, or at minimum control how everyone gets to the vision. That makes sense, and it's so exhausting. Decentralized work requires more trust building on the front end, but ultimately it is easier, more fluid.

Most of the leaders I support in facilitation and coaching are suffering because they are not part of a group that can adapt together. They often express this as a lack of shared skills ("no one else is qualified to work with me") or a lack of funding ("I can't afford qualified staff people"), and those are definitely factors. But in the course of our work together we often find that the deeper problem is in the relationships between the members of the group.

My dream is a movement with such deep trust that we move as a murmuration, the way groups of starlings billow, dive, spin, dance collectively through the air—to avoid predators, and, it also seems, to pass time in the most beautiful way possible. When fish move in this way, they are shoaling. When bees and other insects move in this way, they are swarming. I love all the words for this activity.

Here's how it works in a murmuration/shoal/swarm: each creature is tuned in to its neighbors, the creatures right around it in the formation. This might be the birds on either side, or the six fish in each direction. There is a right relationship, a right distance between them—too close and they crash, too far away and they can't feel the micro-adaptations of the other bodies. Each creature is shifting direction, speed, and proximity based on the information of the other creatures' bodies.

There is a deep trust in this: to lift because the birds around you are lifting, to live based on your collective real-time adaptations. In this way thousands of birds or fish or bees can move together, each empowered with basic rules and a vision to live. Imagine our movements cultivating this type of trust and depth with each other, having strategic flocking in our playbooks.

Adaptation reduces exhaustion. No one bears the burden alone of figuring out the next move and muscling towards it. There is an efficiency at play—is something not working? Stop. Change. If something is working, keep doing it—learning and innovating as you go.

As an individual, developing your capacity for adaptation can mean assessing your default reactions to change, and whether those reactions create space for opportunity, possibility, and continuing to move towards your vision. I am not of the belief that everything happens for a reason—at least not a discernible one; it comforts me sometimes to know there is chaos, there is nonsense. But I believe that regardless of what happens, there is an opportunity to move with intention—towards growth, relationship, regeneration.

Now, as much as I fangirl for change, I still struggle when something that I have planned to be just so changes (did I mention that I am a Virgo oldest child with Aries rising and a Scorpio moon?). I fight until I am exhausted, and then I finally surrender to the inevitable.

I have been working on listening for the opportunity. Often this means I have to have a longer view—time is so good, so consistently illuminating. With time, the apparent crisis becomes a massive blessing. I know this has been true in my life of missed opportunities, heartbreak, organizational shifts, the deaths of loved ones who were miserably and terminally ill. The sooner I can look for the opportunity, the blessing, the more efficient I am in moving towards my vision. The energy it takes to resist and bemoan the change can instead fuel positive movement forward.

A few years ago I received an arts fellowship, which included a weekend of coaching and development,[3] and one of the core messages I left with that weekend is: What is easy is sustainable. Birds coast when they can.

As an individual, get really good at being intentional with where you put your energy, letting go as quickly as you can of things that aren't part of your visionary life's work. Then you can give your all, from a well-resourced place, when the storm comes, or for those last crucial miles.

"Nature has taught me that if humans don't figure out what revolution really means, nature will make the revolution despite us."
—Tawana Petty

---

3   I received the Kresge Literary Arts Fellowship, in Detroit, and the coaching and development was curated by Creative Many and Creative Capital.

This is All the Miracle (Adapting Towards Pleasure)

"I am letting go of pretending that I'm in control."
—Kavitha Rao

It is easy to think everything is a miracle during a moment of external joy—falling in love, welcoming new life into the world, celebrating a major accomplishment, seeing a wonder of the world, being part of a successful march or action… those moments when rightness flows through my body and I feel connected to the great way/force/energy that makes us all one. What is harder is to bring my miraculous perspective to grief, to injustice, to delayed travel, to broken technology, to conflict, to changes of plans, to mercury retrograde—things that can be filed under "bad day" or "bad life."

Mindful adaptation, however, makes it possible to experience the miraculous more often, if not constantly.

· Here's a little story about this:

Once upon a time I was offering an emergent strategy training in Boston.[4]

I was late. Generally I am becoming a late person as I age. I don't want to sound shady, but basically I have been adapting because I was tired of being the only person on time so often.

Kidding!

Mostly kidding…

I haven't fully accepted that I need more time, and slower time, to live my life. I have been trying to adjust around this slower self, so on this particular morning I'd scheduled myself to arrive an hour early.

(I am going to try to tell this story without "bad at math" feelings.)

I knew that the commute to the training was usually forty-five minutes, even with traffic. I left home about fifteen

---

4   This training was hosted by the group Intelligent Mischief, a creative
     design lab for social good.

minutes behind schedule because I was catching up with my mama. When I plugged the address into Maps, it said one-hour, fifteen-minute commute. My gut made the "ruh-roh" sound (my nibbling Máiréad loves *Scooby Doo* so this sound is running fresh grooves in my brain), but my mind overrode that with lots of rational options for the added time, including but not limited to: traffic, the grandiose nature of Boston, how everything in life is a mystery.

As I flew through the tunnels under downtown and my directions said I still had thirty minutes left, my intuition got louder—something is wrong. But I couldn't figure out how to change the situation while moving at that speed without endangering everyone.

Also, I didn't have time to be wrong. I didn't want to be late! So I kept going.

I finally pulled up to what I really wanted to be the Downtown SEIU building where the trainees would be waiting. Instead it was a residential white clapboard house with laundry blowing on the line out front in a near-rural enclave south of the city.

My mind immediately—or finally—conceded to my gut (as opposed to making an argument to go knock on the door), which I appreciated. I figured out that my error was an understandable one—there are two "26 West streets" in Boston. In different neighborhoods. Only one is downtown. Now I was thirty minutes from the training, which was scheduled to start in fifteen minutes.

This is where I adapted towards pleasure.

Well, first I yelled. One good strong wordless yell that filled up the car and released the tension that had been building between my mind and my gut. This is something I have been working on, engaging my anger and actually releasing it in harmless ways when it's live in me.

Then I emailed and called the organizers, to say where I was and to adjust the start time. They didn't sound stressed at all, which helped.

Then I had the thought that often shifts my mood: *this is all the miracle.*

These thirty minutes of being late to a meeting in Boston traffic are being lived by my miraculous irreplaceable body in a dynamic and outstanding system of life moving towards life.

What I mean is, it's my choice… If I spend these thirty minutes berating myself for not triple checking the directions or in some other way not being myself (because most of my stress takes the shape of self attack—"why don't you have a better memory?"; "why don't you prepare your travel better?"; "why aren't you more like [insert superior human of the moment]?"; "why don't you listen to your gut more?"), I will just show up feeling funky, lesser than, and like my precious life has been wasted.

I don't want to waste any of this time.

So I put on Alabama Shakes.

I put "Over My Head" on repeat and I sang it all the way back to Boston.

"The quest is to be liberated from the negative, which is really our own will to nothingness. And once having said yes to the instant, the affirmation is contagious. It bursts into a chain of affirmations that knows no limit. To say yes to one instant is to say yes to all of existence."
—Otto Hoffman, *Waking Life*

Suffice it to say, I arrived at the actual SEIU building for my training feeling gloriously alive, flushed in the cheeks, laughing, clicking together the mind heels of the body in my head that can achieve enough height to click heels together. I walked into the room and… Everyone else was late!

The rest of the day was a shapeshifting adaptation fest.

Emergent strategy is something I am still discovering, but a lot of it, for me, feels like tuning into the natural operating systems of this universe and being humbled, as opposed to trying to barrel through and against all the change, trying to best nature. I am learning to see human behavior, even my own mistakes, as part of a larger natural order.

I am wondering where I have agency, where I am moving and where I am being moved. I keep making decisions and declarations about my life, and then that larger force deftly, elegantly adjusts me on my path.

I keep coming back to response and reaction as the place where I have the most agency, where, as Octavia puts it, I can "shape god." I am moving towards the horizon of the end of my life, I am generating as much liberation as I can on that journey.

I choose what to embody, what to long for, even as the horizon shifts before me. The adaptation is up to me. The laughter between grieving friends, the justice of advancing a righteous anger, the first moments of surrender into new love, the opportunity inside of apparent failure… How often, how quickly can I become aware of the miraculous nature of the moment I am in, and adapt towards the pleasure available in that awareness?

"Your life is your spiritual path. Don't be quick to abandon it for bigger and better experiences. You are getting exactly the experiences you need to grow. If your growth seems to be slow or uneventful for you, it is because you have not fully embraced the situations and relationships at hand. To know the self is to allow everything, to embrace the totality of who we are—all that we think and feel, all that we fear, all that we love.
—Paul Ferrini, found on a sign on the laundry house at Kalani, Big Island, Hawaii

---

Excerpt from *A Framework on Adaptation*

What follows is an excerpt from a piece Movement Generation is developing on adaptation for movements—it feels like a frame that can become common language for looking at the changes we are experiencing. Movement Generation was referenced earlier as the political home of Gopal Dayaneni—it's a circle of humble geniuses studying and teaching complexity, resilience, and organizing in a backyard garden in Oakland.[5]

> Instability has become a defining feature of our times. In many ways, this instability is the new landscape of social struggle. It is useful to classify the economic and ecological disruptions that make up this "new normal" of instability into two groups: shocks and slides.
>
> Shocks present themselves as acute moments of disruption. These are, for example, market crashes, huge disasters and uprisings.
>
> Slides, on the other hand, are incremental by nature. They can be catastrophic, but they are not experienced as acute. Sea level rise is a slide. Rising unemployment is a slide. The rising costs of food & energy are a slide.
>
> While they share a set of root causes, the scale, pace and implications of shocks and slides differ and, therefore require different responses by social movements. One of our key roles, as social movements, must be to harness the shocks and direct the slides—all towards achieving the systemic, cultural and psychic shifts we need to navigate the changes with the greatest equity, resilience and ecological restoration possible.
>
> We define a shift as social, political, economic and/or cultural transformation. From our perspective, we want shifts in the direction of ecological resilience and social equity, as an

---

5   Visit www.movementgeneration.org to learn everything you need to know to live.

imperative. We believe that shifts can emerge from collective "aha" moments when social movements awaken the popular imagination to new possibilities and spark social action. And we are arguing that the coming shocks and slides—if we anticipate and prepare for them properly—can be key opportunities to spark these "aha" moments.

Shifts also result from well-organized communities creating new institutions that meet peoples' needs as responses to the shocks and slides better than the dominant systems can, such as food sovereignty projects, collectivized housing systems, cooperative economics (time banks, worker co-ops, food shares, community-based restorative justice projects, etc.).

"Nature has taught me about fluid adaptability. About not only weathering storms, but using howling winds to spread seeds wide, torrential rains to nurture roots so they can grow deeper and stronger. Nature has taught me that a storm can be used to clear out branches that are dying, to let go of that which was keeping us from growing in new directions. These are lessons we need for organizing. As Octavia taught us, the only lasting truth is change. We will face social and political storms we could not even imagine. The question becomes not just how do we survive them, but how do we prepare so when we do suddenly find ourselves in the midst of an unexpected onslaught, we can capture the potential, the possibilities inherent in the chaos, and ride it like dawn skimming the horizon?"
—Walidah Imarisha, co-editor of *Octavia's Brood*

"We are Earthseed
The life that perceives itself
Changing."
—Octavia Butler, "Earthseed"

Adaptation Example:
How to Facilitate 250 Funders and Organizers[6]

1. For the better part of a year, plan a meeting for 110 funders of social and environmental justice.
2. Two days before the meeting, learn that registration has boomed (or not been closed) and the number

---

6   Notes from my facilitation debrief of the EDGE Funders gathering, April 2016.

of participants has doubled. The new numbers are mostly movement partners—organizers, not funders.

3. On Day 1, name these practices, gathered and/or developed over many months for this experiment, to the overflowing room:
   - less prep, more presence
   - low ego, high impact
   - building alignment, not selling ideas
   - relationship is the measure of our strength
   - this will be as amazing as you are
   - trust your own work and each other

4. Have plenary sessions (plenary simply means that everyone is in one room) that inspire people and point towards the work that exemplifies the vision of the meeting. (Be amazed when speakers respect the amount of time they are given and deliver powerful messages in that container.)

5. Have seven planned breakout "labs"—intimate self-guided spaces where participants can deepen relationships and strategy together by working through shared questions and content. To each lab, assign note takers who will feed the content back to the meeting organizers for weaving throughout the meeting.
   - Have an expectation that rebels will create two or three more labs, no matter how much planning and thought goes into selecting the seven labs.
   - Plan for groups of 10–15 people to struggle and deepen together in these labs. Be flabbergasted when…no one rebels.
   - Because of new numbers and lack of rebellion, support groups of up to fifty people to initially flounder together, then innovate.
   - Forget to set-up a proper orientation for the note-takers, hi-jinx ensue.

6. After the first lab session, invite everyone to be facilitative: keep returning to questions, notice who isn't speaking, let others speak your truth.

7. Encourage innovation and intervention—"do here what we are seeking to do in the world."
   - redirect the energy towards solutions of those who are coming to tell me how badly it's going.
8. Interventions, adaptations. and lessons include:
   - pre-identify facilitators or process people for each session.
   - have an info call before proposals for sessions are accepted (also have a mandatory call to orient facilitators or leaders of session).
   - more curation, rather than simply combining sessions.
   - more deliberate time outside in nature.
   - booking a venue aligned with systems change.
   - be more humane with the venue and event staff.
   - set group agreements before diving into content, offer agreements to the labs to practice in their smaller groups.
   - have agenda reflect focus on building relationships—web information and social media for participants, speed dating.
   - graphic facilitation takes care of lots of ways of knowing, invite artists to capture outcomes.
   - leadership of women is non-negotiable and shifts the results, particularly in the funding world.
   - invite more detailed conversations on how things work, or could work in real world (drop from theory into practice and action).
   - adequate translation/interpretation so that everyone can truly participate.
   - having caucus work can really help—but if it's on side it means extra work. plan for how to weave it in.
   - instead of introductions at the beginning, which no one will remember, have participants say their names as they speak in the room.
   - use small group or fishbowl technology in the labs.

- all change is not systems change or even political change. sometimes positive change upholds the status quo. we are not here to feel good all the time, but to do good.
- remind participants that change happens at a pace relevant for the people involved—we are not ahead of or behind each other, we are in a million experiments.
- participants move between labs but invite them to notice if they are shifting away from something that is their responsibility.

9. Facilitator learnings:
   - relax under pressure! there is no form of freaking out that will make this job less challenging.
   - have a few trusted people/a team to talk to about the challenges.
   - hold a hard line around the self-care basics of sleep and food.
   - continually remind people that on the last day we will get clear on what practices we are taking back into our work and institutions, and how we are turning towards new collective actions
   - have folks partner and share with each other what they are taking home. instead of a list of general tasks that no one claims, generate the next steps from what the people in the room are willing to commit to!

Write up these learnings and share them widely, and with much humility and gratitude to everyone who participated in the grand experiment.

INTERDEPENDENCE AND DECENTRALIZATION:

who we are and how we share

Interdependence is mutual dependence between things. If you study biology, you'll discover that there is a great deal of interdependence between plants and animals. "Inter-" means "between," so interdependence is dependence between things, the quality or condition of being interdependent, or mutually reliant, on each other.[1]

Decentralization: the dispersion or distribution of functions or powers, the delegation of power.[2]

---

1   There were many definitions of interdependence out there—my favorite was this one from vocabulary.com, which also offered this more traditional definition: "a reciprocal relation between interdependent entities (objects or individuals or groups)."

2   *Merriam Webster,* http://www.merriam-webster.com/dictionary/decentralization.

grounding in nature

"I spent an entire year on this porch in Mississippi watching a family of geese. They get to give. Over and over. They get to give. Their style of getting and giving are particular to each bird. But they give every single day. They share and accept sharing with grace and so much style. I'm working on this everyday of my life."
—Kiese Laymon

"When Canada geese are migrating, they take turns at the front of the V—turns being the leader, the weight-carrier, and being the follower, the rester."
—Kat Aaron

When a goose is injured during migration, two geese will land with it and stay until it is healed or it dies, then catch up with their flock. Flocking is fundamentally about decentralizing the effort for safety and trusting leadership to come from any edge of the flock.

"When Hurricane Katrina slammed into the Gulf Coast, almost everything lost its footing. Houses were detached from their foundations, trees and shrubbery were uprooted, sign posts and vehicles floated down the rivers that became of the streets. But amidst the whipping winds and surging water, the oak tree held its ground. How? Instead of digging its roots deep and solitary into the earth, the oak tree grows its roots wide and interlocks with other oak trees in the surrounding area.

And you can't bring down a hundred oak trees bound beneath the soil! How do we survive the unnatural disasters of climate change, environmental injustice, over-policing, mass-imprisonment, militarization, economic inequality, corporate globalization, and displacement? We must connect in the underground, my people! In this way, we shall survive."
—Naima Penniman

Many trees grow from a common root system underground, are one being reaching up in many bodies—birch, ash, mangrove. Oak trees wrap their roots around each other under the earth.

Mycelium, the threading that makes up most mushrooms, communicates between trees, particularly about toxic growth,[3] a process called mycorrhiza.

Most animals, including humans, sustain parasites and bacteria along and within our bodies, some of which manage waste and keep us well.

"Parasites can be symbiotic and help each creature thrive—stronger together rather than divided. Fish cleaning barnacles from sperm whales—cleaner and pilot fish rule!"
—Hannah Sassaman

This support happens between and within species.

---

3   To learn more about this tree-plant communication, see http://www .bbc.com/earth/story/20141111-plants-have-a-hidden-internet.

Ants tell each other where food is, not hoarding individually, but operating on a principle that the more of them that gather the food, the more food they will have as a community.

"In nature everything works in collaboration. There are hummingbirds and flowers that are in such deep coordination they need each other for survival. How vibrant and alive and successful could our movement be if we moved with such coordination and collaboration?"
—Karissa Lewis

"I believe in the honesty of trees. I, like many organizers, have spent a lot of time processing the notion that anything worth its outcome involves everyone's priorities, desires, visions and perspectives in every phase and around every decision. I look at the anatomy of trees as one of nature's examples of successful organizing that realizes that our power is in our ability to both be fiercely centered and grounded but also infinitely reaching towards our unique sources of energy, light, and growth. Each tree's elements are reliant on one another but totally unique in form and function. There is no competition or pressure to be the root or the trunk or the buds that bloom. Each tree is a universe, a master delegator, a puzzle and a puzzle piece. They have encouraged me to not worry so much about making everyone 'feel important' and to focus on how to create systems and support efforts where everyone is important and

clear on how their work is unique, crucial
and totally interconnected."
—Morgan Mann Willis

One of the most common and exciting elements of the vi-sioning exercises I have done with social justice movements and organizations is the desire for a society where there is more interdependence—mutual reliance and shared leadership, vision. This is particularly our longing in the face of economic competition.

Most of us are socialized towards *in*dependence—pulling ourselves up by our bootstraps, working on our own to develop, to survive, to win at life. Competition is the way we hone our skill and comfort with the opposite of mutual reliance—we learn to feel proud about how much we achieve as individuals, and sometimes, to actively work to bring others down in order to get ahead.

In a capitalist society like the United States, every aspect of our survival—from food and water to healthcare, childcare, and elder care—is based on our success at being an individual in the world: *Do we compete well enough to make good money so we can live a good life?*

Competition exists all over nature—being the Alpha is a big deal, competing in mating and survival cycles can be understood as natural. In the absence of reasoning, it appears to be a viable way to manage community power dynamics.

Humans are unique because we compete when it isn't necessary. We could reason our way to more sustainable processes, but we use our intelligence to outsmart each other. We compete for fun, for ego.

The idea of interdependence is that we can meet each other's needs in a variety of ways, that we can truly lean on others and they can lean on us. It means we have to decentralize our idea of where solutions and decisions happen, where ideas come from.

We have to embrace our complexity. We are complex. While many of us articulate a yearning for a more simple life, we continue practicing complexity as our evolutionary path. As I have deepened into a regular meditation practice, and regular retreat times, I have grown an appreciation for simplicity, while also understanding that I enjoy it as a visitation—that being in a complex life is actually intriguing and delicious to my system. And that I have to understand that it isn't just my own complexity at work, but everyone I am in relationship with, creating an abundance of connections, desires, interactions, and reactions.

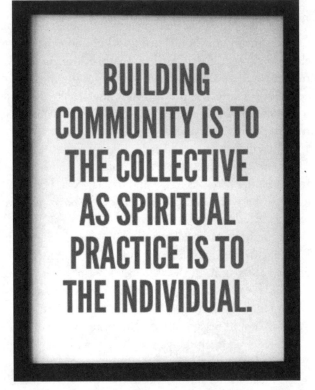

I have begun to wonder how it looks to practice complexity as a sacred path, as interdependence. Of course, whenever I think things like this, I turn to Grace Lee Boggs and find that she was there ahead of me—on the wall of her home is a sign: "Building community is to the collective as spiritual practice is to the individual."

Being a part of movements is complex work, it requires a faith.

a moment for faith

"There are two sayings from the Qur'an/ Islam that have taught me HOW to think about nature as an influence:

"a) 'If only you relied on Allah a true reliance, he would provide sustenance for you just as he does the birds: They fly out in the morning with their stomachs empty and return in the afternoon with full stomachs.'

"This influences my organizing by reminding me that we are not the absolute progenitors of our outcomes. We put in the work, we fly out and we have an intention (get food, end racism, change society, get free) and we work hard, we look for the worms and we build our nests and we fly in formation etc. But at the end of the day we have to believe firmly that there are forces of justice and truth and love at play. We do our part and rely on the greater power of the Universe aka our collective intentions AND efforts. It's relieving to know that it is not always up to us as individuals, but there is a complex interconnection of power at play.

"b) 'A Muslim is like a date palm tree whose leaves do not fall, always beneficial and never harmful.'

"This influences my organizing by reminding me that my core responsibility is to be a benefit to whatever I'm engaged in. I

may not always know HOW that will happen but it has to be my aim. I want peoples' lives to have been better (even in very tiny ways) from having participated with me in this work. This means to me that I bring beautiful words, actions, ideas, and behaviors into spaces. At the end of it all even if we don't see the fruits of our labor, shouldn't we be able to say we loved and enjoyed each other? That's why I want to act and be like a palm tree, providing shade, covering my comrades (instead of throwing shade lol). I want to provide food (dates). I want to be what they can lean on. I want to be a resource, sustaining our work."
—Aisha Shillingford

"I grew up rooted in an early understanding of the continuum between us, the ancestors, and the natural world. Our rituals, medicine, and spiritual guides were all rooted in nature. Ochun represented the sweet waters, Oya the wind, and Orisha Oko, the orisha of agriculture and the fertility of the earth. We were taught all things were interconnected and that we were the keepers of balance. In the Yorùbá tradition, we demonstrate our love for the Creator by caring for Creation. I am a daughter of Ochun and Obatala. You are without a doubt a daughter of Ochun. Listen to 'The River' by Ibeyi."
—Elizabeth Yeampierre

Do you already know that your existence—who and how you are—is in and of itself a contribution to the people and place around you? Not after or because you do some particular thing, but simply the miracle of your life. And that the people around you, and the place(s), have contributions as well? Do you understand that your quality of life and your survival are tied to how authentic and generous the connections are between you and the people and place you live with and in?

Are you actively practicing generosity and vulnerability in order to make the connections between you and others clear, open, available, durable? Generosity here means giving of what you have without strings or expectations attached. Vulnerability means showing your needs.

Love is an Emergent Process

i stand before my love
and let the tendrils unfurl
in every direction
i am whole
and becoming
time is one instance
examining itself
mirrors
seeing each other
and blushing
into eternity

i am the ant
who carries grandfather to the grave
in my palms
you lift the next day's meal
enough for everyone we know
we love in this rhythm
leaving home
and returning
on the wind

love can't look away from itself
vibrating in the cell
fluttering breathless
into sustained migration
i feel you
like dust feels water
and remembers
the home galaxy

it appears nothing is new
never was
and nothing is truly massive
when seen in its wholeness

until i took this breath
repeating the miracle
i didn't know i would say it
could not have known...

i look to the sky
taste the wind on my tongue
and fling myself
into the pattern
when i forget—
when i think the end is near
i realize my insignificance
as important as yours
and begin
to love
again

Interdependence is Iterative[4]

What I have been studying by being hyper-aware inside my life is how much being interdependent is a series of small repetitive motions. Here are some of the things I have had to do repeatedly towards interdependence:

1. Be seen.

Initially with defensiveness (I am not like you say I am) even/especially in the face of experts (I have diagnosed myself, I know what is wrong with me).

And then, perhaps, without agency. Being seen is actually non-negotiable, though I can hide, or I can determine my level of grace and relationship in it. On so many levels, interdependence requires being seen, as much as possible, as your true self.

Meaning that your capacity and need are transparent.

Meaning even when I don't want to look in the mirror, I am (and I choose to be) open to the attention of others.

Sometimes I start with my woes, those with whom I am co-evolving through friendship. I show something I've been hiding, and hope I'm still lovable. This generally goes better than could be expected, every single time.

I have also tried starting out naked on a hard operating table under a bright light, shivering from the cold of so many strangers' eyes.

I can walk towards this "being seen" and experience the beauty of releasing all that guard and protection, that miracle distortion. Or I can resist it and only be seen in moments of trauma and loss of control.

But I will be seen, and the more I open to it, the gentler and more necessary that attention feels.[5]

---

4   I wrote this piece after my ectopic pregnancy in 2015. I wasn't ready at the time to name exactly what had happened—I chose a lesser level of vulnerability that still allowed me to share my learnings about getting my needs met by others.

5   As I was writing this I was reminded that interdependence is basically the song "Lean on Me" in practice: "For/no one can fill/those of your

2. Be wrong.

There is nothing like the wrong feeling of being an intuitive witchy healer and having to be told something indisputable about your body.

Particularly if you've already done the thorough work of disputing said something. Out loud. At a volume that might, by some, be described as unmedicated anguish level. It's pitiful wrong.

The easier "being wrong" is for you (the faster you can release your viewpoint), the quicker you can adapt to changing circumstances. Adapting allows you to know and name current needs and capacity, to be in relationship in real time, as opposed to any cycle of wishing and/or resenting what others do or don't give you.

Sometimes there isn't one definitive truth. (My favorite situations.)

And sometimes there is one and you can't see it. (Least favorite. Least.)

Just at least consider that the place where you are wrong might be the most fertile ground for connecting with and receiving others.

And in a beautiful twist, being soft in your rightness, as opposed to smashing people with your brilliance, can open others up to whatever wisdom you've accumulated. I am grateful to all the people who were softly right about me this past month when I couldn't see my own needs.

3. Accept my inner multitudes.

An honest self would agree to some self-care practice or limitation that would protect my recovering, wounded body. And then another—honest, even earnest—self would almost immediately act against that agreement.

I'd be half bent over to lift something when the voice of one of my precious beloveds would slip through—"Seriously what the fuck are you doing?"

needs/that you don't let show."

(My loved ones are pure molasses sweetness.)

There is a me that wants to get that sugar devil away from me for good. There is a me that can't go through physical trauma without ice cream, can't even imagine that.

The more I accept this, the more I can share my contradictory truths with those who can support me and help me move towards my best self.

I am not turning against myself, I am multitudes. The tide to be turned is a process of inner alignment, those who wish to support me need me to be vulnerable with that inner contradiction.

4. Ask for, and receive, what I need.

Can you drive me to the hospital?

Can you explain what is happening to me?

Can you stop my pain?

Can you open this water bottle?

Can you help me stand up? And sit down?

Can you open the door?

Can you put my bag in the overhead bin?

Can you bring me groceries?

Can you drive me to the airport and actually park and help me bring my suitcase inside?

Can you hold me while I cry?

Can you heal me?

And so on, for what feels like forever…

And most of all, the childlike request inside of story telling: Can you listen while I feel this?

Again?

Again?

I'm learning that interdependence is not about the equality of offers in real time. I had to ask most of these things of people I didn't necessarily know, or who I knew but wouldn't be able to offer anything to in the foreseeable future. I had to trust in that karma-ish idea that the support I've offered in the past, or will offer in the future, would balance this scale, which felt so me-tilted.

Over and over and over I offered up my small self and was held in big ways. Thread through me, again, again.

The result of this experience is that I feel so much more woven into the world. I still anticipate my independence, my default can-do self space. But I don't want to sever any of this connecting fabric between myself and all of the incredible people who held me through this past month, saw me, corrected me, held me in my contradictions, met my needs. I want more of my life to feel this interdependent, this of community and humanity. I love knowing how incredible it feels to have a need met, to be loved and cared for, and also know how incredible it feels to meet an authentic need.

It's data, all this learning. Tender data.

"Patience. The slow painful patience. The one that reminds you to be humble and nimble. The one that reminds you how much existence relies on our ability to remember our connection to earth. We are nature. Not separate or disconnected."
—Patrisse Cullors

"The biggest thing that I've learned from nature is the importance of relationships. E.g. an ecosystem isn't just a list of living things (squirrel, tree, bee, flower); it's the set of relationships *between* those living things (the squirrel lives *in* the tree, the bee *pollinates* the flower). In terms of organizing, this means that a given social movement isn't a list of organizations, or campaigns, or even individuals; it's the set of relationships *between* organizations, campaigns, individuals, etc. Credit where credit is due to the folks at Movement Generation for being the ones who drew my attention to all of this."
—Farhad Ebrahimi

"How do I think Creating Collective Access epitomizes emergence? Innovation, experimentation, relationships. That you couldn't have planned this shit, but it happened because of lots of disability justice work getting the ground ready for this bloom. You couldn't have done any of this from a top down, flow chart, strategic planning meeting in a board room. It happened because three disabled queer people of color trusted our own brilliant knowledge of what we and our communities needed, our own resources we already had to do it, and reached out, with love, to each other."

—Leah Lakshmi Piepzna-Samarasinha[6]

Confessions of a Charismatic Leader in Recovery

"There is also the danger in our culture that because a person is called upon to give public statements and is acclaimed by the establishment, such a person gets to the point of believing that he is the movement."

—Ella Baker

"We are all connected. Like our bodies, if one single molecule is off, then our entire bodies are affected. In nature, if one thing is off balance, then we are all off balance. Organizing from this

6 For more information about Creating Collective Access, read Leah's full piece on Creating Collective Access at alliedmedia.org/ESII and/or check out three years of archived posts at https://creatingcollectiveaccess .wordpress.com.

perspective allows us to see that it's not enough
for any one of us to be ok if others are in dis-ease."
—Rusia Mohiuddin

"Nothing happens in isolation. There is always
a squad, collaborators, a body that supports
change occurring."
—Sage Crump

So. In an interdependent movement, with decentralized innovation and leadership—how do we respond to the gift and
curse of the charismatic leader?

In my political education, I learned how the civil rights
movement had been negatively impacted by the same charismatic leaders who so inspired me. When leaders became visible, whether beloved or controversial or both, they became
endangered politically and physically, which led to assassi-
nations—tragic losses that left vulnerable movements. There
was an apparent leadership vacuum that slowed momentum
for years—I say "apparent" because there were tons of leaders
who survived that time, but they didn't play as well to the
media, or didn't want to. Many of them didn't fit the mainstream idea of what leadership looked like (male, straight,
loud, individualistic, articulate, handsome, charming, etc.).

I have heard the stories from elders, stories about how the
non-movement public perceived an absence of leadership,
how that *perception* shook the movement's self-perception.

Of course movement analysis of what happened within
movement space is more nuanced—patriarchy, educational
privilege, colorism, and other factors played into the tensions
that weakened movement during that time. And—in the
spirit of nonlinear and iterative change, I would say that the
civil rights movement did exactly what it could do based on
what was known and possible at the time.

Many of us have experienced the trials and tribulations of the charismatic leader in movement today. Or the flip side: trying to lead an effort and generate resources for work when you don't quite fit the bill of a charismatic leader, or when you have a big personality but just don't feel comfortable in that position (me).

Being anointed as a movement rock star at any scale can be confusing, trust me.

On one hand it's like—Yay! Baby, I'm a star!

This can be healing, especially for those of us who experience being invisible to the world. I went from being a nerdy fat girl in glasses to a fabulous! brilliant! badass! nerdy fat girl in glasses—because I gave one really fantastic speech to a room full of people with influence and resources in the movement. Now—maybe it was a truly fantastic speech. Maybe it was just that I tapped into my life force, my magic, for the first time publicly—at least, it was the first time I can remember feeling the sparkle at the base of my skull that tells me the room is opening, that anything can happen.

I thought I alone made that magic feeling! I've learned a lot since then.

I learned, because there is always the other hand: rock stars get isolated, lose touch with our vulnerability, are expected to pull off superhero work, and generally burn out within a decade.

No one has time for rock star tears.

I have talked with other leaders who got bumped into rock star status as young organizers and almost all of us share a few core experiences: People stopped seeing us. We became a place to project longings and critiques. We lost touch with the fact that it's ok to make mistakes. Then we made the biggest mistakes of our lives. And we learned the hard way that rock star status is a cyclical thing. It becomes its own work, maintaining and promoting the rock star in the organization.

The work of promoting and protecting one personality is as different from the work of organizing as holding one's breath in is from an exhale.

And then the transitions are a mess! Many of us have seen or lived through the emperor-has-no-squad moment when a great organization was ready for the first leadership transition and it became clear that all the greatness was largely perceived to come from the founder.

Lifting people up based on personality replicates the dynamics of power and hierarchy that movements claim to be dismantling.

So. I have some charisma, I know. I am trying to only use it for good, while also building up my practices of authenticity that can balance the instinct to "glamour" people.[7] The first step is awareness.

When a charismatic leader finds the right place for their work, they, we, can be quite useful. I have seen leaders move into politics, media, and art, using their skills in those arenas to raise the profile of movement work. In my own work, as a facilitator and a writer, I have intentionally put myself in positions where no organization's income depends on the whims of my personality. We work well when we have people we are accountable to, people with whom we can be in interdependent relationships.

Otherwise we are monsters. We can make missions drift, can get embroiled in inter-organizational or inter-movement beef that does not serve the people, can get into a victim mentality and direct a lot of movement energy towards defending our egos, or get convinced of our superiority.

Mostly, we can get too isolated for accountability.

If you are in a leadership position, make sure you have a circle of people who can tell you the truth, and to whom you can speak the truth. Bring others into shared leadership with you, and/or collaborate with other formations so you don't get too enamored of your singular vision.

The Social Transformation Project has been doing a variety of experiments in creating safe spaces for leaders to be

---

7   Awesome term from *True Blood* for manipulating people away from their self-knowledge.

vulnerable and speak honestly of their accomplishments, failures, longings, and where they want and need collaboration. generative somatics is also cultivating authentic presence and relationships amongst movement leaders. BOLD does this for Black leaders. Having these spaces and others is helping movements develop a new definition of a great leader—not just one who is inspirational in speech or grand actions, but one who is inspirational in collaborative action, accountability, and vulnerability.

One more thing to add: Whether a leader is great or not, funders have traditionally preferred the narrative of a rock star leader, and have invested in individuals more than in missions. The people of an organization make or break the work, and the best mission will not be realized without the right people behind it. The shiny stars are rarely the ones actually getting the work done, or even doing the most exciting thinking in the organization.

If you are in the funding world and your primary relationship with those you fund is with the executive director, if you have not had a meaningful conversation with other staff members or community members, you may be stricken with charismitis—relational laziness induced by charismatic brilliance.

It's ok, it happens to everyone. But you can unlearn this behavior! Edge Funders, Resource Generation, and Building Equity and Alignment are three formations working to shift this and other donor/funder malpractice.

Finally, if you love a charismatic leader and are trying to increase accountability with them, be willing to stand next to them in honest relationships, and be willing to name the power dynamics (repeatedly if need be). Part of how I became aware of myself was through co-directorship with Sharon Lungo and Megan Swoboda at The Ruckus Society. We worked together until they no longer needed my charisma, they had their own magic and systems and strength. Here is some wisdom from them directly:

"Our survival depends on the relationships we build. Some relationships are utilitarian—and sometimes that's okay. If I can be useful to others, I should be. I am not important, but what I do—and don't do—matters. My actions and inactions affect everyone and everything around me. We all play our role. None is more important than the others. But we all affect each other. Some roles and strategies seem insignificant or ineffective, but all together—all our different tactics and strategies and roles *can* get us what we need to survive, and thrive. But it is not a sure thing. We must fight for it."

—Megan Swoboda

"Water has been my greatest teacher—partially because I am a woman and it is a strong medicine that I carry, but also because of its sheer power. It has taught me to reflect on my own participation in work, taught me to remember the fundamentals that life is built on. That things cycle, that nothing is ever truly finished, so we have to stay vigilant and aware of how things move, even when we think we win. Lastly, water has taught me that with enough force and will, I am unstoppable."

—Sharon Lungo

NONLINEAR AND ITERATIVE:

the pace and pathways of change

---

nonlinear: not denoting, involving, or arranged in a straight line.[1]

iterative: involving repetition, as
    a: expressing repetition of a verbal action
    b: relating to or being iteration of an operation or procedure.[2]

---

grounding in nature

Many of us have heard some version of the butterfly effect—that a butterfly flaps its wings and it sets in motion a series of escalating changes and reactions that lead to a hurricane. This is also called chaos theory—the study of behavior and conditions of dynamical (changing) systems that are highly

---

[1]   *Oxford Dictionaries*, https://en.oxforddictionaries.com/definition/us/nonlinear.

[2]   *Merriam Webster*, http://www.merriam-webster.com/dictionary/iterative.

sensitive to initial conditions. There is chaos, there are cycles, there are winding paths— each change process is unique.

"Nature has taught me so much about moving with the seasons, that we need to honor times of harvest and times of rest. That the frenetic pace of doing, doing, doing, without being present with each other and the season we are in, what is happening around us, is unnatural and counter to life. So it has made me realize how important community ceremony and celebration is to our efforts to transform the world."
—Brenda Salgado

"From its own fetal curves, green fiddleheads produce ancient spiral formations. The fiddleheads teach me to unfurl my own lineage & experience patterns—examine them, be with them, and listen to their messages. The fiddleheads are gifted time-travelers. If I don't learn the lesson now, the pattern will show up in my life like an unwelcome visitor. By meditating with the spiral in mind, I can focus my attention on re-encountering the old wounds differently and imagine a new possibility. The fiddleheads teach me the vitality of a perspective shift. The fiddleheads teach me to respect the slowest micro-movements & and own my way forward."
—Marie Varghese

"Climbing Poetree's Naima Penniman asked, 'I wonder … if compost believes in life after death.' Like compost, our

work is not linear in a static timeframe. Not discounting set goals and objectives, compost has taught me how to reflect and grow from an action or effort in organizing beyond the breadth of conventional expectation. Our successes can be measured more than one way. How did we learn from our hiccups, errors, mistakes, fuckups, drama, and difficulty that goes into an action, our 'shit'? How can future generations learn from and build on what we do, our work and intentions now?"
—Sierra Pickett

"The universe is both orderly and chaotic. We understand it to a point, and then there is mystery. And that is not linear or cumulative. There is no eventual elimination of mystery. There will always be mystery. And knowledge. Humans are both understandable and mysterious. Communion is all about acceptance, and organizing is about both."
—Peter Hardie

Transformation doesn't happen in a linear way, at least not one we can always track. It happens in cycles, convergences, explosions. If we release the framework of failure, we can realize that we are in iterative cycles, and we can keep asking ourselves—how do I learn from this?

Emotional growth is nonlinear. It feels really important to me to include pieces on grief and emotions in this book because, as people participating in movements, we are faced with so much loss, and because we have to learn to give each other more time to feel, to be in our humanity. Not to come to a standstill as a movement, but to take turns actually feeling what is happening to and around us, and letting our feeling help us understand what we must do. Because that is what we are creating, a world where we can feel ourselves and each other and do less harm and generate more freedom.

As movements are made up of humans, movement growth is also nonlinear. There are two major movement cycles that I want to uplift here, Occupy and Black Lives Matter/ Movement for Black Lives, as recent nonlinear organizing processes that started off to speak to class and race intersections in the US, respectively.

Both grew from common longing, from a relinquishing of control, and from a celebration of leaderfull transformation. Both have been challenged by the limits of our human capacity to cooperate, sustain, and grow in conflict; by the weight of large-scale expectations on something long awaited but new; by the learning pains of organizing for depth in the age of social media. However these are the most exciting mass movements I have lived through, and are both part of any justice we are creating.

In a non-linear process, everything is part of the learning, every step. That includes constructive criticism, it is part of the feedback loop—experiment, gather feedback, experiment again. This is how we learn.

That said, the line between constructive critique and hater is a hard one to navigate. In this section I will also offer a protocol for haters, who are the least useful parts for movement building and social transformation.

A Time Traveling Emotion

in the moment, i was not ready to feel the feeling, my skin too firm, my faith too solid. when the future all seemed ahead of me, it was easier to fold an emotion into me and believe it was gone, or at least silenced.

when my feelings started to work their way back out of me, to the surface, i was overwhelmed. i put my hands over my mouth to hold it in, but it didn't matter, i was brimming, screaming.

i am not the only one like this, it may be a human condition, or an empath condition, or a Black girl magic. it may even be an epidemic of consciousness. i am not convinced we get to know that.

but in my twenties, when i was gutshaking about things that were leaping out of me like emo tweens, that's when i learned about the time traveling emotion.

it is like anything else that traverses time, both fully of another time and fully present in the place when it appears. in the case of grief, the time traveling emotion touches into your sadness over a present day experience of absence, and then drags forward a living satchel of the most tender innocent moments, the smallest memory. or perhaps sucks your heart back in time.

my grandfather, impossibly big and godly, hugging me, in his own garage, just out of the near-georgia sun, with the smell of hay and horses around us. it isn't just the senses, but the complex spectrum of a moment completely felt.

the more i learn to feel, the less time it takes a time-traveling emotion to catch me. years instead of decades, hours instead of months, seconds instead of weeks.

i am even learning, sometimes/more often, to feel in real time. and to survive feeling a whole emotion in real time.

with less shame, i say no to anything that wastes my time. i gather and give myself hours that belong to no one else, alone or with healer types. i claim time when i can be in my body and self. and in that solitude, or healing company, i become a defined place for a time-traveling emotion to locate, an x on the nonlinear map of my emotional life.

the emotion is a living thing—showing one face when it arrives, and as it leaves i see it's really a pattern, delta-ish, blood in veins connecting aspects of myself as disparate as lung and toe.

music is one of the systems by which emotions traverse time, both in tone, content, and something as simple as age. some emotions stay in the soundtrack of their root memory. there is a janet jackson song that opens the way to an emotion of innocence. a new song can surprise me when it opens the way to something dusty and eager to be felt.

each time-traveling emotion softens me, especially those that return often. it's so humbling to feel something in spite of logic, time, circumstance, and thinking the feeling is finished. grief is a sharp visitor, her long nails a surprise in my chest. heartbreak is heavy and fireworky, like full-body tears, swollen eyes. joy melts my jaw.

it's all waves though, moving towards and up, through and beyond. and once i've survived an emotion that has reached across time to demand my attention, i feel so resilient. that resilience makes me soft and wide enough to handle the complex mercurial existence of the present moment.

i trust myself to feel, to grow from what i feel, not to run when i sense a feeling coming.

i am a student of this phenomenon that makes time a shape shifter. i still fold moments of particular intensity into me. but now i do so with a bit of a spell attached: i promise, i will be ready for you when you find me.

"Life is a matter of a miracle that is collected over time by moments, flabbergasted to be in each other's presence."
—Timothy "Speed" Levitch, "Waking Life"

Spell for Grief or Letting Go

Adequate tears twisting up directly from the heart and rung out across the vocal chords until only a gasp remains;

At least an hour a day spent staring at the truth in numb silence;

A teacup of whiskey held with both hands, held still under the whispers of permission from friends who can see right through "ok" and "fine";

An absence of theory;

Flight, as necessary;

Poetry, your own and others, on precipice, abandonment, nature, and death;

Courage to say what has happened, however strangling the words are...and space to not say a word;

A brief dance with sugar, to honor the legacies of coping that got you this far;

Sentences spoken with total pragmatism that provide clear guidance of some direction to move in, full of the tender care and balance of choice and not having to choose;

Screaming why, and/or expressing fury at the stupid unfair fucking game of it all (this may include hours and hours, even lifetimes, of lost faith);

Laughter, undeniable and unpretended;

A walk in the world, all that gravity, with breath and heartbeat in your ears;

Fire, for all that can be written;

Moonlight—the more full the more nourishing;

Stories, ideally of coincidence and heartache and the sweetest tiny moments;

Time, more time and then more time...enough time to remember every moment you had with that one now taken from you, and to forget to think of it every moment;

And just a glimpse of tomorrow, either in the face of an innocent or the realization of a dream.

This is a nonlinear spell. Cast it inside your heart, cast it between yourself and any devil. Cast it into the parts of you still living.

Remember you are water. Of course you leave salt trails. Of course you are crying.

Flow.

P.S. If there happens to be a multitude of griefs upon you, individual and collective, or fast and slow, or small and large, add equal parts of these considerations:

- that the broken heart can cover more territory.
- that perhaps love can only be as large as grief demands.

- that grief is the growing up of the heart that bursts boundaries like an old skin or a finished life.
- that grief is gratitude.
- that water seeks scale, that even your tears seek the recognition of community.
- that the heart is a front line and the fight is to feel in a world of distraction.
- that death might be the only freedom.
- that your grief is a worthwhile use of your time.
- that your body will feel only as much as it is able to.
- that the ones you grieve may be grieving you.
- that the sacred comes from the limitations.
- that you are excellent at loving.

From Liberty Plaza[3]

Yesterday I got to Liberty Plaza, finally.

Since it came to my attention I have been making my way towards it, wanting to see it and feel it myself, though with some trepidation. I tend to roll with a critical crowd, and I have to work hard sometimes to keep my heart open when there are lots of critical questions sitting there for me to ask:

Is it a bunch of privileged white kids?
Is it stinky dropouts?
Is it a mash-up of wingnut messaging?
Is it our tame Tahrir square?

Or…
Is it the decentralized movement we have been
    awaiting?
Is it safe for queer people, people of color, for me?

---

3   I originally published this on my website on October 9, 2011 after visiting the Occupy Wall Street encampment at Liberty Plaza (Zuccotti Park). See http://adriennemareebrown.net/2011/10/09/from-liberty-plaza/.

Is it rooted with existing movements for economic justice?

I had to know.

So I went. Getting off the train at Wall Street there is
immediately a little hand-written, taped up piece of paper
pointing towards Zuccotti Park. First I walked around the
perimeter, lined with people facing outward with signs,
taking in the love, admiration, disrespect, insults, and ignorance of the passersby with a generally curious and
calm presence.

I wound my way through the inner park, taking in all the
systems and offerings and community there, as well as hundreds of others like myself, come to see and feel this massive
cultural happening. I saw a few folks I knew, but they were
also there seeing how to plug in. That excited me.

What I felt there was a resounding yes, yes to all of my
questions, and many more.

More precisely, what I felt was the surge of energy I used
to get at a march, realizing that there were so many people
wanting change, people who had walked completely different
pathways to reach the same conclusion that they were willing to give their precious lifeforce to changing the systems
of our time.

This has the potential to be deeper, because it feels less
fleeting, less temporary, less spectacle. Marches have left me
feeling so unheard for so long.

Here, I noticed the wingnut messaging, and the whiteness…and yet I felt close to tears a few times, seeing unexpected diversity in the crowd, seeing the self-organized systems
emerging for creation of art, sharing of information, health,
and wellness. There was even a table of "coaches" to help people figure out what their role in the movement could be.

No one is special, and everyone is needed.

To speak to the whiteness of the crowd, I actually felt moved
to see so many white people, very normal-looking white

people, standing around the edges of this park looking liberated themselves, holding up signs that criticize capitalism.

Some were speaking from their privilege, and others from their own economic struggles. But to have masses of white people in the streets talking about the economy with a progressive decentralized grassroots perspective, and have it not be the Tea Party, is a tipping point signal.

The crises are becoming clear even to those not being directly oppressed, or those directly organizing. And people are ready to stand up and dream of something different.

And yes of course it would be amazing to see even more people of color there.

My sense was that we need only show up, in whatever capacity we can, and there we will be. There is also a case to be made for white privileged folks sleeping in the park to hold space for people of color and poor folks who may not have the luxury to drop work and do so, but are in alignment. Solidarity can look so many different ways.

It's movement.

I have been in movement spaces for a long time, and we have a way of doing things that is so steeped in critique that I have often wondered if we would strangle movement before it could blossom. Sometimes I think we put up the critiques to excuse ourselves from getting involved, and sometimes I think we do it to protect our hearts from getting broken if it doesn't work out. Critique, alone, can keep us from having to pick up the responsibility of figuring out solutions. Sometimes I think we need to liberate ourselves from critique, both internal and external, to truly give change a chance.

The major critique I have heard of this effort is the lack of demands, and multitude of messages.

My thought so far is: humans have a multitude of cares, of passions…trying to lockstep us into one predictable way of being is the essential desire of corporations, because if you can predict what people will want and do, then you can profit by coming up with appropriate products and activities for them. This movement is instead making it as easy as possible to enter, no matter what passion brought you to the square.

And in terms of the demands, it seems the central demand is to build and expand a conversation that is long overdue in this country, a conversation that doesn't have simple cut and dry demands. We are realizing that we must become the systems we need—no government, political party, or corporation is going to care for us, so we have to remember how to care for each other.

And that will take time, and commitment, a willingness to step outside of the comfort of the current and lean into the unknown, together. To listen to each other across all real and perceived divides.

I have heard stories of folks having issues, bringing them to general assembly, and being able to shift the process, even as newcomers. I have seen random people call for the people's microphone, and others—including myself—jump in to spread the message, regardless of the message.

The whole thing seems so utterly not produced, not micromanaged, and not acting from a place of crisis which excuses top down elitist decision-making processes—not rushing itself.

I see this as a natural evolution from conversations and gatherings and organizing that has been building for years, call and response across time from the battle in Seattle, the street forums that take analysis beyond the choir.

It's taken a long time to get to this place. Now it's time to let the fruit burst on our tongues and savor the flavor of something tangible that we grew with our courage to hold the line against the inhumanity of corporate greed. Let's spend less time on the imperfection of the process, and more time articulating and crystalizing our lessons.

Liberty Plaza is important, the call to Occupy Wall Street is important.

And like any anti-Zionist American with an analysis of imperialism here at home and abroad, I don't love that this proliferation of events is naming themselves "occupy 'insert city."' I get it. We are going to occupy America with justice, to take up the space of being in this country, in these cities and in these banks, be vocal occupants of this place, reshaping it to something that yields solidarity in place of shame.

I love the other options I am hearing: "Decolonize 'insert city'"; "Occupy within"; and "Foreclose 'insert institution.'"

It feels spacious. It feels like something you can do, no matter where you are, by authentically applying yourself to the changes you wish to see. At Liberty Plaza, it is a physical occupation. In Detroit, it may be a massive redistribution of food and shelter resources heading into the winter. Tomorrow I will get to see what it looks like in Oakland.

Don't sit this out. It has room for you. Find out, start, or help shape what is happening in your town.

Let It Breathe[4]

Moved to write more…

Just home from Occupy Oakland, and hearing reports from the first general assembly meeting in Detroit. Last night I heard from folks who had gone to check out Occupy SF, and I am following the budding of several cities in their parallel efforts.

In each instance there are various levels of excitement and disappointment.

There is such urgency in the multitude of crises we face, it can make it hard to remember that in fact it is urgency thinking (urgent constant unsustainable growth) that got us to this point, and that our potential success lies in doing deep, slow, intentional work.

We need to go beyond having a critique/counter analysis/alternate systemic plan for society—we have to actually do everything differently, aligned with a different set of core principles for existence.

---

4   This piece was originally published at http://adriennemareebrown .net/2011/10/11/let-it-breathe/, October 11, 2011.

Especially our movement building.

How do we live compassion, justice, love, accessibility, in alignment with this planet and with the people on it? How do we live our values?

As we are, so it (our work, our movement) will be.

For the majority of us, myself included, this means vast ongoing transformation from how we are currently living and being. And as we transform, we see more things that need transformation, within ourselves and the world.

It is so important to cultivate our patience, our thoughtfulness, our willingness to slow down and seek the wisdom of those not already part of our movements—not to get them in step with our point of view, but because we need their lived experiential wisdom to shape solutions that will work for the majority of living beings.

It is imperative to regenerate our curiosity, our genuine interest in different opinions, and in people we don't know yet—can we see them as part of ourselves, and maintain curiosity, especially when we want to constrict and critique?

Can we each take our little spark from the fire that has started and truly let it breathe enough to grow?

Occupy Wall Street didn't start off as big as it is now; it started small and built community, cultural norms, and communication… And it's still building.

The challenge in other cities is that we are all starting off with a lot more people at the table with ideas and directions and agendas to push.

That means time spent on getting a clear decision-making process in place will be worth every second in the long run.

That means facilitators skilled in consensus and synthesis have an important role to play.

That means that individuals and organized bodies with all variety of experiences are showing up, and we have to humble ourselves to value all contributions, from the newest people to the most organized professionalized folks.

That means our socialized practices to control each other and compete are going to emerge, and we have to be attentive and accountable as we try to open ourselves to something larger than our particular formation or analysis.

That means we can do, be, and create whatever we want to see, knowing ours is one effort in the midst of many, and the multitude is where our power lies.

Before joining Occupy Oakland folks today, I got to witness two incredible presentations on movement and network building at the Engage Community of Practice gathering I am facilitating.

One of them, from Jenny Lee, offered a key metaphor that is used at Allied Media Projects: the role of organizers in an ecosystem is to be earthworms, processing and aerating soil, making fertile ground out of the nutrients of sunlight, water, and everything that dies, to nurture the next cycle of life.

All that has come before is in the soil, which now yields the movement to counter Wall Street and the systems of capitalism and create a new economy of relationships, a new society of care and respect.

In that paradigm there is no failure.

Everything we attempt, everything we do, is either growing up as its roots go deeper, or it's decomposing, leaving its lessons in the soil for the next attempt.

Another lesson I observed from the people's mic experience at Occupy Wall Street...if someone called for the mic, they were granted it. But if people weren't feeling the statement, eventually they stopped repeating it.

I shared that observation with Jenny and she observed that in a way, twitter has prepped us for this succinct and self-selected rebroadcasting of each other.

And just like with the people's mic, and our social media efforts, what we pay attention to grows. Let's cultivate the movement we want, and leave space for others to do the same.

There's room. Let it breathe.

"We're basically this very young species, only 200,000 years old. We're one of the newcomers,

and we're going through the same process that other species go through, which is, how do I keep myself alive while taking care of the place that's going to keep my offspring alive?"
—Janine Benyus

A Protocol for Haters

As much as we, who do and/or fund social and environmental justice, speak of movements, when they actually spark, many of us cannot tolerate all the newness and unknown that comes along with scaling up our efforts to create change. We want instant order, more familiarity, a perfect plan for all of eternity, a set of lock-step agreements to either adopt or reject.

We can also be quite vicious when movements appear from places we weren't looking. Zuccotti Park and Ferguson, MO were not hotbeds of movement investment and organizing at the moments when they became the locations for historical change. And with both Occupy and Black Lives Matter, a lot of people who didn't create the movement moments had a

when are we

When are we
I feel I, we, all mine
Are lost in time
They raised the battle flag
In Avon Minnesota today
To show the borderlessness
But we already knew
Everywhere is war
But when
And why
Do we hear bugles
Do we smell smoke
When we hug Black bodies?
Oh, the church is on fire
No another one
No another one
No another one
No another one
No another one
No…another one
It's those ghosts again
Their children's children are
Non-linear haunts

But
Isn't this the future
How are a million eyes open
But no one will look…
When can we run go hide
When are we
These days of ashes
We wake up wary
Which illusion is killing us
Which construct
Is it our flesh hunted
Or our time
Each moment fills up with
  smoke
We are catching fire
Again
We feel the rocking of ships
The grief of the sea
We stumble
We moon walk in chains
We dance free
But when could we
Just be

LOT to say, a lot of critiques on what the movements were not doing and/or needed to do.

Sometimes it is hard to see that ongoing movement work is always in the soil of new and rapid growth. And sometimes it is hard to admit that, for all our strategizing, we weren't the ones to articulate the moment. Sometimes, it can make us into haters.[5]

I have been disappointed by how many "movement" haters there are, how many people have attacked these movements on sight. Or more precisely, these movement cycles, because this is all part of a larger, ongoing intersectional many-headed movement towards justice and liberation.

There are way too many people in critique mode who belong to no formation, who spend their lives writing volunteer think pieces in 140 character bursts of Internet. It makes me feel defensive of the messy chaotic beauty of transformation. Uprisings and resistance and mass movement require a tolerance of messiness, a tolerance of many, many paths being walked on at once.

I feel in me a movement doula energy—the baby knows exactly what it needs to know, it is doing what it is meant to do. Babies don't learn to eat or poop in a toilet or walk instantly, it is slow, iterative, repeating attempts fueled by curiosity and longing. The parents know what they need to know, and are learning what they need to learn. Parents don't know how to raise a child because they read all the books and went to the classes. They figure it out in the dead of night, covered in shit and tears and finally holding the sleeping child, stunned by love.

I have an inner protocol in my doula work with parents and babies: ask myself if I am needed, support only as needed, do absolutely everything that is needed (change the diaper, sweep the floor, rub mama's feet, take out the trash—no task is menial), and make space for the natural order to emerge.

---

5   "Hater: A person that simply cannot be happy for another person's success. So rather than be happy they make a point of exposing a flaw in that person."—www.urbandictionary.com

I offer, from this defensive and sacred place, a protocol for those who are most comfortable approaching movements from a place of critique, AKA, haters.

1. Ask if this (movement, formation, message) is meant for you, if this serves you.
2. If yes, get involved! Get into an experiment or two, feel how messy it is to unlearn supremacy and repurpose your life for liberation. Critique *as a participant* who is shaping the work. Be willing to do whatever task is required of you, whatever you are capable of, feed people, spread the word, write pieces, make art, listen, take action, etc. Be able to say: "'I invest my energy in what I want to see grow. I belong to efforts I deeply believe in and help shape those."
3. If no, divest your energy and attention. Pointing out the flaws of something still requires pointing at it, drawing attention to it, and ultimately growing it. Over the years I have found that when a group isn't serving the people, it doesn't actually last that long, and it rarely needs a big takedown—things just sunset, disappear, fade away, absorb into formations that are more effective. If it helps you feel better, look in the mirror and declare: "There are so many formations I am not a part of—my non-participation is all I need to say. When I do offer critique, it is from a space of relationship, partnership, and advancing a solution."
4. And finally, if you don't want to invest growth energy in anything, just be quiet. If you are not going to help birth or raise the child, then shhhhh. You aren't required to have or even work towards the solution, but if you know a change is needed and your first instinct when you see people trying to figure out how to change and transform is to poop on them, perhaps it is time you just hush your mouth.

As Detroit movement ancestor Jimmy Boggs taught, "It is only in relation to other bodies and many somebodies that anybody is somebody. Don't get it into your cotton-picking mind that you are somebody in yourself."[6]

We are all learning what it means to be somebodies who shape the future, to operate at the scale of transformation.

---

6   Grace Lee Boggs, *Living for Change: An Autobiography* (Minneapolis: University of Minnesota Press, 1998).

RESILIENCE:

how we recover and transform

Resilience: The ability to become strong, healthy or successful again after something bad happens. the ability of something to return to its original shape after it has been pulled, stretched, bent, etc. an ability to recover from or adjust easily to misfortune or change.[1]

"**Resilience:** (v) The way the water knows just how to flow, not force itself around a river rock; then surely I can stretch myself in the shape my own path is asking of me."
—Corina Fadel

---

grounding in nature

"Everything, given time and nurturing, is moving toward balance and healing. The mushrooms that cleaned the land after nuclear trauma...the process of forest growth after a fire...the way our skin heals after a

---

1   *Merriam Webster*, www.merriam-webster.com/dictionary/resilience.

cut...stronger than before. Healing is organic, healing is our birthright."
—Lisa Thomas Adeyemo

"Nature regenerates. It works in unison in its creation & destruction. Nature is a collective entity. It lives on no matter what, in oceans, forests, volcanoes and shifting tectonic plates, in the sighs of tigers and the hum of birds wings. Nature heals itself."
—sham-e-ali nayeem

"From Starfish I have learned that if we keep our core intact, we can regenerate. We can fall apart, lose limbs, and re-grow them as long as we don't let anyone threaten that central disc's integrity. We can grow so many different arms, depending on what kind of sea star we are. We have to nourish ourselves with the resources we are surrounded by, with our community assets if you will, and by doing so we help keep ecosystems delicately balanced."
—JoLillian T. Zwerdling

"Nature is in the pesticides that are in the flesh of whales in the deepest parts of the arctic ocean, because what humans create is not exceptional, it is not outside of nature.[2] The vastness of the cosmos is a nuclear reactor that creates all the elements that make us up and makes up our minds and all that we create, from poetry to weapons, sweatshops and digital networks

---

2   This made me think of Anohni's lyric on *Hopelessness*: "Why did you separate me from the earth?"

made in them that connect people. Nature is everything."
—micha cárdenas

"We are part of this universe; we are in this universe, but perhaps more important than both of those facts, is that the universe is in us."
—Neil Degrasse Tyson

"Nature reminds me that healing is natural. My body, spirit, and mind want to heal and I need to create the space and time to do that."
—Andrea Quijada

Mushrooms detox the soil around them, not just removing the toxins, but transforming toxic content into nourishment.

After many dives I now think of "coral reef" as a verb, or a process, a way that ocean life creates home and beauty out of ships, cars, bikes, and other things never meant to live on the ocean floor.

The very cycle of food and nourishment in nature, the food chain, which works because most things on earth can be food at some point in their lives or deaths. All of the creatures I grew up disgusted by—roaches, mosquitos, rats, vultures, squirrels (in a trashcan there is no difference between a rat and a squirrel)—have slowly gained my respect because of the breadth of ways they nourish themselves, their adaptive survival brilliance.

"When I was young I was taught to fear big forces of nature—tornadoes,

thunderstorms, snowstorms, hurricanes.
Taught they cause destruction and
devastation. Taught to hide under desks,
in basements, stay close to home. For me,
somatic work has been about relearning
and reconnecting to the wisdom and life in
natural forces. That what is most alive leads
to opening, creating, change. That in the
destruction of something lies a whole new
world of possibility—a place where patterns
can finally become unhinged and there's
space for something new to take its place.
Not that this doesn't come without loss, grief,
devastation, it often does. But to see that
there's also resilience, the beauty of survival,
the move to create and thrive despite what
surrounds us. To me that's the essence of our
fights for liberation."
—Spenta Kandawalla

Humans, especially humans who persist in trying to trans-form the conditions of life, are remarkably resilient. We experience so much loss, pain, hardship, attack—and we persist! Resilience is in our nature, and we recover from things that we would be justified in giving up over, again and again.

Resilience is unveiled when we are triggered, injured, heartbroken, attacked, challenged. I am curious about our general resilience as social justice actors in a traumatizing world, and as collectives of people shaping the next phase of human evolution. One core practice of resilience is transformative justice, transforming the conditions that make injustice possible. Resilience is perhaps our most beautiful, miraculous trait.

i am not afraid
of what i came here to do
i'm made of stardust
we are not afraid
of what we're called now to do
we're all made of god

Human Nature in Futbol

I am not generally a futbol (or any other kind of sports) watcher. Sports are so oriented around competitive and capitalist indulgence, uplifting heroes and gathering faceless erasable masses to cheer them on.

But I am beginning to suspect that nothing operates outside the realm of emergent strategy.

I was in Amsterdam during the World Cup. It was part of being immersed in this place, sitting at coffeeshops with my lover and watching the competition with an international spread of locals.

I didn't have a particular team I was rooting for, and really only engaged around the quarter finals, but once I got hooked I couldn't stop watching. And rather than rooting for particular teams or players, I was fascinated by the patterns and rhythms, the art of the game—it looked like movements. So I want to offer some analysis from my non-expert vantage point.

I was watching the semi-final match when Germany scored seven points on Brazil, most of those points within an eighteen-minute free for all in the first half. It was brutal to see.

I had the humbling opportunity, during my dad's last assignment in Germany, to be a fairly useless part of my high school soccer team. We were invited to play a friendly international match against a team of German third graders. They scored like thirty goals on us while barely seeming to move or break a sweat. Over and over they took the ball away while we ran in circles, gasped for air and tried not to cry.

I didn't understand why Brazil looked like my high school team. In the semi-finals of the World Cup! I needed it explained to me. I was reaching out to people, because the commentary was in Dutch and I needed to know where the gorgeous warrior dancing magicians I'd witnessed in the quarter-final against Colombia had disappeared to.

My sister Autumn reminded me that, in that very breathtaking match, Neymar was injured, and Silva was carded. She broke down how much Neymar and Silva were the center-captain-irreplaceable aspects of offense and defense, respectively.

Watching the end of the World Cup, it occurred to me —first as I found myself hoping for a mercy ruling in the Brazil–Germany match, and then again while watching Germany seem to easily work together to defend and score on Argentina in the final—that this was a perfect example of emergent strategy in action.

Emergent strategy includes being intentional, which, at a basic level, I think all of the teams were. They each intended to win number one, period. But it also includes being intentional even in a fractal sense, at the smallest level. Watching the way Germany had one to two people in pursuit of the ball even when the opposing goalie was trying to figure out where to kick it, there was a hungry focus on possession of the ball that presenced their intention to win in even the smallest moments.

Emergent strategy includes being decentralized. Brazil's team was oriented around key stars who embody certain skill sets. When those players are in and on, it is the most beautiful playing I have ever seen. For Germany's team, even after watching them play several games, I couldn't point out anyone irreplaceable on their team, any superstars or best players. Based on my limited viewing, they seemed to easily interchange players and fluidly move together to defend their goal—not as dazzling, but consistent, effective, beautiful in its collectivity.

Emergent strategy is adaptive and interdependent. When Neymar and Silva were taken out, Brazil didn't have the capacity or depth on their team to adapt. The lack of cohesion from their team felt loud. Germany moved like a flock of birds over and around the field. They worked as one body to take possession of the ball and move it. Any time Brazil or Argentina got the ball, Germany suddenly had four players around them. It didn't feel like a formation, it felt like interdependent murmuration towards a shared intention—they flew towards the ball. The sheer number of team members attending to the ball at any given point meant that Germany was consistently creating more possibilities for itself to have the ball, to have choice over what happened next, to get the chance to score.

"For me it sometimes doesn't feel so easy to pause, center, and listen to nature's messages. Let's be frank—organizing can be chaotic and exhausting. But nature has taught me that while chaos exists we can always have balance. I am learning to listen to those resiliency messages from nature, in the same ways that I have learned deep authentic listening as a part of how I organize. When the balance is off or chaos enters, elements of the ecosystem fail, life is harmed, relationships are damaged, sacrifices are made, new ways of being emerge. Nature makes shifts to resist, rebuild, restore, and create. It strives towards balance, wholeness by being in togetherness and harmony with each other."
—Beatriz Beckford

How We Learn From Pain

"If we are going to heal, let it be glorious."
—Beyoncé

"You don't need to use force to defend yourself—safety can come in hiding in yourself like a turtle, or hiding by being yourself in the right place, like a praying mantis, invisible on a green branch (or a toad fish on the sea floor), or by doing something unexpected like an armadillo (they can jump three feet straight up in the air to startle predators, and then they run away!)."
—Kat Aaron

"*Dii Nvwati* (Cherokee). Translation: Skunk medicine. The skunk asks us to defend ourselves effectively, without causing further conflict. Self-protection but do no harm. Gangsterish peace-making. That is the kind of masculinity that I try to embody. With my leadership, with my poise, with my privileges. As my body continues on a journey of thickening, muscle hardening, limbs lengthening, Ayurvedic drying, shorter synapse pathways, fuzzier intuition, and choppier verbal articulation all facilitated by weekly testosterone injections these are poignant lessons to forward. The objective is for men and masculine people to not yield our power to others... Women and femme people don't need our paternalistic sickle to swath as we 'tap out.' We must figure out power without domination.

"Just as our body mass of people of color in the United States continues to grow and we inch near the time of outnumbering the current White majority in population numbers it will be imperative that we use our people power strategically. Numbers alone won't ensure justice and liberation. The skunk asks

us to use our powers effectively, without wiping ourselves out. Without recapitulating top down, give-less-to-get-more social structures. Just as the skunk does not seek to be the bear, let us not attempt to trade places with the oppressor. Let us navigate a road of paradigm shifting that seeks to salve both current social and economic injuries, but also prepare a sustainable method of being for seven generations to come."
—Holiday Simmons

"And then there is the butterfly, a most magical creature. The wings of the butterfly are already held inside the caterpillar, and as it breaks down its old self into goo the wings emerge ready to go. That process is amazing and teaches me that as we change and transform, we also have everything we need already right inside of us. So my organizing and healing work becomes about building the cocoon that can hold the goo so that the wings can emerge."
—Micah Hobbes Frazier

Nothing in nature is disposable. Part of the resilience of nature is that nothing in nature is wasted. The earth swallows it all through mouths or soil or water. This is such a simple beautiful truth. Everything is food, fuel, compost, a home for some other creature.

There are predator and prey dynamics in nature, there are battles over territory. There are systems and power dynamics. There is a focus on mating and the rearing of offspring. There are reasonable and unreasonable behaviors. There are toxic materials, there are volcanic explosions and avalanches and so much destruction. And yet nothing is disposable, the cycle of life ultimately makes use of everything.

"I've found that our immediate environments are mirrors for the spiritual turmoil inside of us that we inherited from our forebears. By reclaiming our relationship with the Earth, we can then start healing ourselves and our communities from the inside out and from the ground up."
—Shane Bernardo

Humans have made of ourselves a hierarchy of value in which some people are disposable—can fail at being human, can be killed as a punishment, can be collateral damage. Can be wasted. Or tortured. Or locked in a small box for their whole lives, given no hope of transformation, or a future in society.

And even those of us who critique these punitive methods, who are committed to justice, practice our own versions of prisons, blacklists, takedowns, and public executions. When we don't agree with each other, we destroy each other. When we feel competitive with each other, we splinter and... destroy the other. We say we don't care, and then invest time and energy into cultivating conflict with each other. When we feel scared, we destroy each other instead of working to get to the root of our fear.

How do we shift into a culture in which conflict and difference is generative?

One place to turn to with a transformative justice lens is our shared vision. When we imagine the world we want to shift towards, are we dreaming of being the winners of the future? Or are we dreaming of a world where winning is no longer necessary because there are no enemies?

Domination or peace? I argue that peace is the most strategic option for our long-term survival. Not an uninformed or compromising peace—a peace that is built on truth, accountability, and equity.

I will admit here that even some of my closest loved ones find me naive for holding a vision of a humanity with no enemies. I *can* imagine it though, and in fact, it seems like the only viable long-term solution. We need to transform all of the energy we currently put into war and punishment into creating solutions for how to continue on this planet. The time, the energy, the money—we actually have all of that in abundance. What we lack is will.

What we put our attention on grows.

We have been growing otherness, borders, separateness. And in all that division we have created layer upon layer of trauma and vengefulness, conditions for permanent war, practices that move us into a battle with the very planet we rely on for all life. The scale of division, conflict, racism, xenophobia, and hierarchical supremacy on our planet is overwhelming.

Finding the places of healing and transformation, moving towards a world beyond enemies, is work that has to be done for our survival. Which means transformative justice—justice that transforms the root causes of injustice—is necessary at every scale, but I am particularly focused on how it becomes the common orientation and practice of movements for social change, for peace, for liberation.

I tie transformative justice into emergent strategy because it feels like a non-negotiable aspect of our future, and because the natural world has guidance for us here.

Transformative justice, in the context of emergent strategy, asks us to consider how to transform toxic energy, hurt, legitimate pain, and conflict into solutions. To get under the wrong, find a way to coexist, be energy moving towards life, together.

While we often put our attention on the state and demand transformative and restorative justice, it is important that individuals begin practicing in our personal, familial, and communal lives—we can reach the people we need to reach, and measure our work by the way the relationships feel. It is hard work, but it is accessible to anyone, anywhere, at any scale.

Eventually, transformative practices that begin small will demand new societal structures. I suspect we can't back into this, demanding that our government provide a form of justice that even we in our movements do not know how to practice in real time. So let's grow our expertise in this.

Before I go any further in this section, I want to share with y'all some wisdom from the incomparable Shira Hassan.

Shira and I can never quite remember when and how we met, but it was when we were both doing harm reduction work—reducing the harm from drug use and sex while increasing the agency of each human being to make decisions related to his/her/their body without shame or judgment.

And we were thrilled to find each other.

Over the years, she has been a confidante, tarot reader, guide, friend—she has taught me how to be less judgmental, to love my fatness, to embrace my own needs as my body has gone through various levels of ability and disability, and, through her work at Young Women's Empowerment Project (YWEP) and her consulting, she has taught me a ton about transformative justice. I showed Shira an early draft of this book and her feedback was so good that I had to include it here as a core part of this chapter. Here is some Shira brilliance:

> I love that you are writing about transformative justice in the context of emergent strategy. I need us to acknowledge more that we have no idea what we are doing—that we are birthing a new collective consciousness out of the pain of losing too many people to colonialist justice. I need transformative justice (TJ) to be framed as a part of emergent strategy so that we can acknowledge we are midwifes to a changeling—that TJ is mutable process with only its values set in stone. In order to resist one size fits all justice, we have to resist the idea that every process looks the same. The goal is for us to embody these values so that our creativity can guide our healing and our

drive for treating each other with true justice. With every experience of healing on our own terms, we also begin to heal the generational wounds of colonialist justice.

Here is the definition I use in my trainings and that YWEP used too:

Transformative Justice:
1. Acknowledges the reality of state harm.
2. Looks for alternative ways to address/interrupt harm, which do not rely on the state.
3. Relies on organic, creative strategies that are community created and sustained.
4. Transforms the root causes of violence, not only the individual experience.

I love the piece you wrote that is included later in this section ("We Are Still Beginning")—it's one of my favorites on TJ right now and I've been using it in my workshops.

"Nothing in nature is disposable"—this isn't most people's belief—I just killed a bug earlier today and will set out some rat poison tomorrow… lol—but for real… also the struggle between disposability and getting something/someone that doesn't work for me out of my life.

No one is disposable and yet—we have a right to make boundaries. Furthermore, we want people to make boundaries.

For people who are currently in abusive situations and living with their violent partners, this kind of TJ thinking needs more clarity. I can't tell you how many times I have had to go back to the drawing board because someone I love has used TJ principles of transformation and non-shaming to justify the return of their abusive jerk partner. I say all this to say I think its important to think of the audience as people who are currently in abusive situations—what are we telling them? What are we asking?

I really like Generation 5's work on this—I use this a lot—it is a combination of gen5's principles with YWEP's thinking combined into it:

Safety, Healing, and Agency For All

1. Safety, Healing, and Individual Agency for Survivors.
2. Accountability and a transformation for people who harm.
3. Community action, healing, and/or group/ org accountability.
4. Transformation of the social conditions that perpetuate violence.

Lessons From a Transformative Breakup: How to Find New Ways to Be In Each Other's Lives and Not Split the Communities We Love or the Movements We Support

Try every single thing you can to make it work, and articulate the effort you are making to each other. Even things you aren't sure will work—try EVERYthing. This will matter later.

Love yourself.

Don't let fear make you settle for something you know isn't working.

Be honest. The harder things are to say, the more necessary they are to say.

Commit to being in each other's lives, and doing whatever is needed to ensure that in the long term.

…This may include being far away from each other (physically, and in social media, and in all communications) in the short term.

Set boundaries around communication and stick to them. This includes how often to communicate, what is ok to talk about, who it's ok to talk to about the process, and permission to express feelings. You can identify a new boundary as you go along if something hurts or doesn't feel right.

Don't tell anyone else until you are ready.

Be intentional about who you tell, what you say, and letting people know what is and isn't ok to talk or ask about. Write a letter to your community if need be. That way your true story trumps gossip and bullshit.

Feel your feelings.

Feel your feelings!

Feel your feelings.

Gather trusted support around you and lean on them as much as necessary.

Together, tell the story of your relationship to a trusted and neutral friend. What happened, what was great, what did you learn? Be as honest as possible, and take the time to tell the whole thing.

Don't judge each other's choices, feelings, or processes. You can't actually know what is going on for the other person. Take responsibility for your own feelings and act accordingly.

When you feel ready, dream together about the new relationship you want to have with each other.

As you come into new, post-breakup relationship with each other, watch for your patterns and take it slow.

Celebrate your maturity and growth and ability to be present and do this.

Invite others to celebrate and applaud the efforts.

When you feel ready, enjoy the friendship you made possible together.

Please note: All of this is in the case of a generally awesome, healthy relationship that doesn't quite work—not an abusive one that you may need to actually completely leave quickly.

Transformative Justice In An Abusive Dynamic

"Like everything in nature, we all have gifts.
Sometimes the gifts don't seem like gifts, the
bee that stings, the stinging nettle that irritates
your skin. But when we look at our ecosystem in
totality it is clear how each piece is necessary for
the whole. It's a reminder to make room for all of
us, in all our fiery, stinging glory."
—Karissa Lewis

"Every living thing has a role in the ecosystem
and its own destiny to fulfill—even things we can't
see, don't like, or don't understand."
—Judy Hatcher

When an abusive dynamic builds between lovers, family, partners, or coworkers, it is first and foremost important to understand that it is a dynamic that both/all parties are playing into, consciously and unconsciously. This is different from an abusive event—one explosive moment. This is when there is habitual emotional, spiritual, and/or physical violence and cruelty.

An abusive dynamic is sustained by the two or more people directly involved in it, and a bevy of others who ignore, enable, or exacerbate it.

When we are children or dependents, we don't usually have full agency to shift or leave an abusive dynamic because our safety and livelihood depend upon our abuser, and many of us figure out other ways of "leaving"—dissociation, appeasing, addiction, etc.

When we are adults, we can begin to notice how we are playing into the dynamic, and to shift. We have agency, even if we feel like we are solely victims. That realization can be liberation itself.

Often the same dynamics echo across different realms of our lives—what we allow in our home and love realm shows up with our friends, or with our families, or with our coworkers, bosses, or partner organizations. It is our pattern, our shape.

These patterns are prevalent within our movements, spilling the boundaries of our personal lives and creating toxicity in our organizations and networks. We perpetuate abusive dynamics under the guise of accountability, call-outs—even solidarity and love.

If you have the ability to see the dynamic, to see yourself in a pattern, and walk away before reaching the point of emotional or physical harm… Bravo!

And if not, hey—most of us don't. We need community to hold us in our dignity and to support transformative justice.

Here are a few signs that you may be in an abusive movement, work, family, friendship, or romantic dynamic:

- you make agreements or set boundaries and they get crossed or broken, *and/or* you can't hold the agreements/boundaries yourself.
- you can't communicate directly with the person/people about issues or concerns (culture of gossip usually grows here, in the family, office, group).
- when you raise the issue that agreements or boundaries are not being held, there is no accountability (the other person or people deny the transgression, say they forgot the agreements, say it is your fault, ridicule you, continue the transgression—*and/or* you can't see your accountability in boundary crossing, and/or diminish the harm).
- there is a culture of blaming or dishonesty that breaks down trust over time.
- you don't feel comfortable processing the issues of the dynamic with friends, coworkers, allies (you feel ashamed, or like it will upset the other person/people in the dynamic).
- arguments are really confusing and/or repetitive—you

can't tell what you are arguing about, the arguments
have no boundaries or containers, you keep returning
to issues you felt were resolved, or you keep losing
track of your own values and center in the process.

- you feel dismissed, hidden, or disrespected, *and/or*
  like you can't acknowledge reality, be transparent, or
  respectful.

- you feel like a core part of yourself is compromised or
  not welcome, *and/or* you want to change a core aspect
  of another person or group.

- you feel bullied or bullying, scared or scary, emotionally unsafe.

- you feel like something is being taken from you, *and/
  or* that you are taking from the other person.

Once you become aware of the dynamic, it is important
to take some space to get clear in yourself. So often these dynamics perpetuate because we are scared to be alone, scared to
create conflict, scared to take a step back. And then once we
do, we get more air, more clarity.

If it feels like there is work that can be done for mediation, healing, and transformation, by all means put time
and attention there, but with some humility—the nature of
abusive dynamics is that they are foggy and hard to navigate
from within. Often we leap to couples therapy or office mediation while still in the private fog of it all. Get transparent
and current with trusted friends or comrades who can offer
perspective on the situation.

You have the right to tell your story. The silence and
shame around these dynamics makes people think they are
alone and especially flawed. Not so. Organizations are rife
with abusive bosses or collective members, social justice
movements are full of couples in private battles against the
oppressive dynamics we face in the world. You are not alone,
and you do not have to be silent.

You do not have the right to traumatize abusive people, to
attack them personally or publicly, or to sabotage anyone else's

health. The behaviors of abuse are also survival-based, learned behaviors rooted in some pain. If you can look through the lens of compassion, you will find hurt and trauma there. If you are the abused party, healing that hurt is not your responsibility and exacerbating that pain is not your justified right.

You do have the right to walk away, to literally and virtually gather yourself up and remove yourself from the dynamic. Take space in order to remember and fortify yourself.

You have the right to create boundaries that generate more possibilities for you. Those boundaries may be short term or permanent.

You have the right to ask for support from your friends/ community. It really helps to find neutral mediators, or mediation teams, to support conversations that the abusive dynamics may make difficult. Sometimes the feeling of things being unresolved will keep pulling you back into the conversation—mediation can help draw the line.

You are not obligated to engage in a process with someone if you do not feel like it—whether you feel unsafe or exhausted or angry. While we are working towards a world where all conflict can be resolved in a transformative way, we aren't there yet, and a lot of messy shit goes down in the name of transformative justice. One thing to really track here if you are the abuser, or in a mutually abusive dynamic, and you don't want to participate in a process—this could be you dodging responsibility that, if you did take it on, could transform your life and future relationships. But it's up to you.

You have the right to not know the right moves to make.

"I remember as a small child seeing the geese flying south. Firefly season. A cicada that lived for a while in the cracks of the cement bricks that made up our porch wall. A flash flood sweeping cars away while we were huddled under an overhang on a picnic. Lightning felling a tree in our backyard. I guess I learned that everything will pass.

"But also, and equally true, it will all come back again."
—Karen Joy Fowler

Liberated Relationships

One of the fastest ways to learn interdependence is to shift how we show up in relationship. Primarily, to get more honest in our relationships. I am not saying you especially are a liar—I am saying we are a culture of liars. We learn to lie, either with overt mistruths or egregious omissions, at a very intimate level, not to ask for what we need, not to say aloud what we want, not to be honest when things hurt or bother us.

Here are some reasons we swallow our truths:

- Capitalism: we are taught that love is about belonging to one person or community, and we must contort in order to ensure continued belonging. We are taught that our value is in what we can produce, and emotions impede production.
- The oppression of supremacy: we are taught that, if we are not white, male, straight, able, wealthy, adult, etc., our truths don't matter. This starts very early, we are taught that our feelings and thoughts as children are unimportant, that we are to "be seen and not heard."
- The oppression of false peace: we are taught that our truths are disruptive, and that disruption is a negative act. This one is particularly insidious, and ties back into capitalism—only those moving towards profit can and should create disruption, everyone else should be complacent consumers.

For these reasons and others, we stay in the realm of repressed emotions and passive or outright aggression, and we end up in personal and professional relationships that don't serve us. Because we are fractal creatures, these patterns repeat in every part of our lives. To close the gap between what we actually want and need and what we communicate to others, we have to be in the practice of authenticity in relationship, or what I am calling Liberated Relationship. Here are some of the principles in development for Liberated Relationships:

- Radical honesty. No omissions, no white lies, no projections. Ask the questions you really want answered, speak your truth, and let the relationship build inside all that reality. Just a note from experience, the small lies can be the hardest to stop telling. "No I don't want to get on the phone right now, can we just text?"; "I'm busy catching up on my reality TV show"; "Real cow milk ice cream"; or "I know I said I didn't want to ___, but now I do." However, the more you practice this, the more you will find yourself spending your waking hours in the ways you want to, the ways that honor the miracle of your existence, which was not given to you to waste in polite avoidance of hurting people's feelings. You will find that you can be honest and kind, you can be honest and compassionate.
- Acknowledge the dynamics, then keep growing. Have an understanding on the front end of the race, class, gender, ability, geographic, and other power dynamics that exist between you. And also remember that these are constructs. Be in the complexity of living inside these constructs while evolving beyond them through relationship.
- Relinquish Frankenstein. You are not creating people to be with, or work with, some idealized individuals made of perfect parts of personality that you discovered on your life journey. You are meeting individuals with their own full lives behind and ahead of them. Stop trying to make and fix others, and instead be curious about what they have made of themselves.

Ok do you want to try Liberated Relationships? I suggest starting with one and building from there. Pick one person who is in your life right now, someone you want a more authentic relationship with, and tell them exactly that. Ask if you can practice radical honesty together. It is difficult at first, but the results are unparalleled freedom and satisfaction.

As you grow this skill, bring it to work, to family, to love. I have found that I now spend immensely less time managing the truth for others, and have people around me who want and encourage the real me to show up. In the practices section check out "Coevolution Through Friendship and Woes."

We Are Still Beginning[3]

I've been thinking a lot about transformative justice lately.

In the past few months I've been to a couple of gatherings I was really excited about, and then found myself disappointed, not because drama kicked up, which is inevitable, but because of how we as participants and organizers and people handled those dramas.

Simultaneously I've watched several public takedowns, call-outs, and other grievances take place on social and mainstream media. Some of those have been of strangers, but recently I've had the experience of seeing people I know and love targeted and taken down. In most cases, very complex realities get watered down into one flawed aspect of these people's personalities, or one mistake or misunderstanding. A mob mentality takes over then, an evisceration of character that is punitive, traumatizing, and isolating.

This has happened with increasing frequency over the past year, such that I'm wondering if those of us with an intention of transforming the world have a common understanding of the kind of justice we want to practice, now and in the future.

---

3   Published at adriennemareebrown.net, and edited for *Makelshift* 18 (December 2015).

What we do now is find out someone or some group has done (or may have done) something out of alignment with our values. Some of the transgressions are small—saying something fucked-up, being disrespectful in a group process. Some are massive—false identity, sexual assault.

We then tear that person or group to shreds in a way that affirms our values. We create memes, reducing someone to the laughingstock of the Internet that day. We write think-pieces on how we are not like that person, and obviously wouldn't make the same mistakes they have made. We deconstruct them as thinkers, activists, groups, bodies, partners, parents, children—finding all of the contradictions and limitations and shining bright light on them. When we are satisfied that that person or group is destroyed, we move on. Or sometimes we just move on because the next scandal has arrived, the smell of fresh meat overwhelming our interest in finishing the takedown.

I say "we" and "our" intentionally here. I'm not above this behavior. I laugh at the memes, I like the apoplectic statuses, the rants with no named target that very clearly critique a specific person. I've been examining this—why I can get caught up in a mob on the Internet in a way I rarely do in life (the positive mob mentality I participate in for, say, Beyoncé or Björk feels quite different, though I know there is something in there about belonging…eh, next book). I have noticed that at the most basic level, I feel better about myself because I'm on the right side of history…or at least the news cycle.

But lately, as the attacks grow faster and more vicious, I wonder: is this what we're here for? To cultivate a fear-based adherence to reductive common values? What can this lead to in an imperfect world full of sloppy, complex humans? Is it possible we will call each other out until there's no one left beside us?

I've had tons of conversations with people who, in these moments of public flaying, avoid stepping up on the side of complexity or curiosity because in the back of our minds is the shared unspoken question: when will y'all come for me?

I have also had experiences where I absolutely wanted to take someone down, expose them as a liar, cheater, manipulator, assailant. In each of these situations, time, conversation, and vulnerability have created other possibilities, and I have ended up glad that I didn't go that route, which is generally so short-term in its impact. Sometimes this was because transformation was possible between us. Sometimes this was because the takedown wouldn't have had the impact I wanted; destroying a person doesn't destroy all of the systems that allow harmful people to do harm. These takedowns make it seem as if massive problems are determined at an individual level, as if these individuals set a course as children to become abusers, misogynists, racists, liars.

How do I hold a systemic analysis and approach when each system I am critical of is peopled, in part, by the same flawed and complex individuals that I love? This question always leads me to self-reflection. If I can see the ways I am perpetuating systemic oppressions, if I can see where I learned the behavior and how hard it is to unlearn it, I start to have more humility as I see the messiness of the communities I am part of, the world I live in.

The places I'm drawn to in movement espouse a desire for transformative justice—justice practices that go all the way to the root of the problem and generate solutions and healing there, such that the conditions that create injustice are transformed.

A lot of people use these words, and yet...we don't really know how to do it.

We call it "transformative justice" when we're throwing knives and insults, exposing each other's worst mistakes, reducing each other to moments of failure. We call it "holding each other accountable."

I recently reposted these words from Ryan Li Dahlstrom, speaking about this trend in the queer community:

> I'm feeling really tired of the call out culture on social media especially within queer/trans people of color communities. We need to

center and build relationships with one another and not keep tearing one another down
publicly without trying to have direct conversations. While there are many places of learning,
growth, and contradictory practice within the
world we live in, why can't we talk to one another directly and allow room for learning from
our mistakes or differences? By making these
public attacks on each other, we are engaging
in the same disposability politics of capitalism and the prison industrial complex that we
purport to be against while feeding into state
surveillance tactics that are monitoring how we
are tearing each other down. Enough is enough
y'all. We need each other now more than ever.[4]

Yes, Ryan Li, I too am tired of it. But I see it everywhere I turn.

When the response to mistakes, failures, and misunderstandings is emotional, psychological, economic, and physical
punishment, we breed a culture of fear, secrecy, and isolation.

So I'm wondering, in a real way: How can we pivot toward practicing transformative justice? How do we shift from
individual, interpersonal, and inter-organizational anger toward viable, generative, sustainable systemic change?

In my facilitation and mediation work, I've seen three
questions that can help us grow. I offer them here in context
with a real longing to hear more responses, to get in deep
practice that helps us create conditions conducive to life in
our movements and communities.

1. Why? Listen with "Why?" as a framework.

People mess up. We lie, exaggerate, betray, hurt, and
abandon each other. When we hear that something bad has

---

4   This quote was originally posted on Ryan Li Dahlstrom's Facebook
     page and is shared with permission.

happened, it makes sense to feel anger, pain, confusion, and sadness. But to move immediately to punishment means that we stay on the surface of what has happened.

To transform the conditions of the "wrongdoing," we have to ask ourselves and each other "Why?" Even—especially—when we are scared of the answer.

It's easy to decide a person or group is shady, evil, psychopathic. The hard truth (hard because there's no quick fix) is that long-term injustice creates most evil behavior. The percentage of psychopaths in the world is just not high enough to justify the ease with which we attempt to label that condition to others.

In my mediations, "Why?" is often the game-changing, possibility-opening question. That's because the answers re-humanize those we feel are perpetrating against us. "Why?" often leads us to grief, abuse, trauma, often undiagnosed mental illnesses like depression or bipolar disorder, difference, socialization, childhood, scarcity, loneliness. Also, "Why?" makes it impossible to ignore that we might be capable of a similar transgression in similar circumstances. We don't want to see that.

Demonizing is more efficient than relinquishing our world views, which is why we have slavery, holocausts, lynchings, and witch trials in our short human history.

"Why?" can be an evolutionary question.

2. Ask yourself/selves: What can I/we learn from this?

I love the pop star Rihanna, not just because she smokes blunts in ball gowns, but because one of her earliest tattoos says, "Never a failure, always a lesson."

If the only thing I can learn from a situation is that some humans do bad things, it's a waste of my precious time—I already know that.

What I want to know is: What can this teach me/us about how to improve our humanity?

What can we learn? In every situation there are lessons that lead to transformation.

3. How can my real-time actions contribute to transforming this situation (versus making it worse)?

This question feels particularly important in the age of social media, where we can make our pain viral before we've even had a chance to feel it. Often we are well down a path of public shaming and punishment before we have any facts about what's happening. That's true of mainstream take-downs, and it's true of interpersonal grievances.

We air our dirt not to each other, but with each other, with hashtags or in specific but nameless rants, to the public, and to those who feed on our weakness and divisions.

We make it less likely to find room for mediation and transformation.

We make less of ourselves.

Again, there are times when that kind of calling out is the only option—particularly in relation to those of great privilege who are not within our reach.

But if you have each other's phone numbers, or are within two degrees of social-media connection, and particularly if you are in the small, small percentage of humans trying to change the world—you actually have access to transformative justice in real time. Get mediation support, think of the community, move toward justice.

Real time is slower than social-media time, where everything feels urgent. Real time often includes periods of silence, reflection, growth, space, self-forgiveness, processing with loved ones, rest, and responsibility.

Real-time transformation requires stating your needs and setting functional boundaries.

Transformative justice requires us, at minimum, to ask ourselves questions like these before we jump, teeth bared, for the jugular.

I think this is some of the hardest work. It's not about pack hunting an external enemy, it's about deep shifts in our own ways of being.

But if we want to create a world in which conflict and trauma aren't the center of our collective existence, we have to practice something new, ask different questions, access again our curiosity about each other as a species.

And so much more.

I want us to do better. I want to feel like we are responsible for each other's transformation. Not the transformation from vibrant flawed humans to bits of ash, but rather the transformation from broken people and communities to whole ones. I believe transformative justice could yield deeper trust, resilience, and interdependence. All these mass and intimate punishments keep us small and fragile. And right now our movements and the people within them need to be massive and complex and strong.

I want to hear what y'all think, and what you're practicing in the spirit of transformative justice. Towards wholeness and evolution, loves.

CREATING MORE POSSIBILITIES:

how we move towards life

Create:
1. to cause to come into being, as something unique that would not naturally evolve or that is not made by ordinary processes.
2. to evolve from one's own thought or imagination, as a work of art or an invention.[1]

Possible/possibility: that may or can exist, happen, be done, be used, etc.[2]

Wavicle: an entity having characteristic properties of both waves and particles.[3]

The **multiverse** (or **meta-universe**) is the hypothetical set of finite and infinite possible universes, including the universe in which we live. Together, these universes comprise everything that exists: the entirety of space,

---

1   *Dictionary.com*, http://www.dictionary.com/browse/create.

2   Ibid., http://www.dictionary.com/browse/possible.

3   *Oxford Dictionaries*, https://en.oxforddictionaries.com/definition/wavicle.

time, matter, energy, and the physical laws and constants that describe them.

The various universes within the multiverse are called "parallel universes," "other universes," or "alternate universes."[4]

---

grounding in nature

"From dead plant matter to nematodes to bacteria, never underestimate the cleverness of mushrooms to find new food!"
—Paul Stamets

"Last weekend I went on walk with my partner at the arboretum. There's this little makeshift stream and all the trees along the stream had their roots in the stream. It just makes me think of how that happened and how long it would have taken for the roots to reach there and how that tree had to survive before it reached the stream. This helps me think about how, when we feel limitation, this is when we figure out how infinite our possibilities for us to grow out, around, thru to reach abundance."
—Chrislene DeJean

"I've learned to trust nature. If she can make my weirdo, genderqueer, capable self, she can make anything. Nature helps me reimagine and reform justice and hope like the ocean reimagines and reforms

itself when it washes back in from sand/
mountains, faucets."
—Jay-Marie Hill

"The plant people have taught me to be
generous and not be shy about blossoming,
that it is our nature. I think when others
see us, it can inspire them to open up and
blossom too and we can be a field ablaze
with dignity and beauty together."
—Brenda Salgado

Biodiversity is a beauty of the natural
world, the variety of life. Whether you take
the planet as a whole, or the ecosystems at
a smaller scale—a forest, a pond, a puddle—
life is constantly creating options. In our best
human practices, we watch the systems of
the world and follow them—permaculture.
The natural world manifests life in ecosystems, not monocultures. One of my favorite
ways of understanding nature creating more
possibilities, is to watch water move through
the world. Water creates the ways for itself,
moving with gravity, moving around obstacles, wearing down obstacles, reshaping
the world. When there isn't an overt way
forward, water seeps into the land, becomes
a vapor in the sky, freezes into ice. When the
time comes, water moves over the land in
cloud form and nourishes elsewhere. And,
of course, we humans are mostly water. And
look how many ways we manifest.

"I've always been drawn to the water: oceans,
lakes, rivers. In recent years, I've come to

recognize how this deep, spiritual connection to the water energy connects me to the rhythms of our planet and our peoples—it is a necessary form of healing. Living cradled in between the mighty Mississippi and the beautiful Gulf of Mexico, their water strength provides me constant nourishment. I've learned from this that my organizing practice must include healing, as nature's energy is one we can always tap into when we feel depleted or overwhelmed. Sometimes tides are high, and sometimes tides are low, but the waters remain in balance. And so can we. For me, to stay in the struggle for the long haul and keep going for another twenty years, this is critical."

—Jayeesha Dutta

"I am a priest of Yemoja—the ocean is sacred to me. It's my place of worship, of home, of grounding. If I am drowning in my own stuff, because of the relationship I have with Yemoja, she reminds me that my salvation is in moving the way she moves. The ocean doesn't stop moving—it moves in different ways, with different levels of intensity—Coney Island looks one way, the Indian Ocean moves another more ferocious way, it's still all the ocean. Yemoja reminds me to not get caught up with this external calendar of production, or get caught up with the idea that visibility is the same as doing the work. When I am flowing and can hear that small but powerful voice say 'yes,' I feel a complete sense of calm, I know I am heading in the right direction."

—Joan Morgan

"If Mama Nature teaches us nothing else, she teaches us that diversity is absolutely necessary for survival. Now, she doesn't mean some surface diversity, but a system where every single being is doing their part, pulling their weight. A homogenous, 'gentrified' eco-system would quickly die. If we are committed to organizing sustainable and liberating social movements they must be diverse, pulling especially from those who are the most impacted instead of suppressing their voices or using them as props."
—Nia Eshu Robinson

"The world we want is one where many worlds fit."
—Zapatistas

"When forced into a binary, you always choose wrong."
—Jelani Wilson

Creating more possibilities is my favorite aspect of emer-gent strategy—this is where we shape tomorrow towards abundance. Creating more possibilities counters the very foundational assumptions about strategy.

The word "strategy" is a military term, which means *a* plan of action towards *a* goal. I want to really emphasize the "a"s in that sentence—there is a practice of narrowing down, identifying one path forward, one strategy, one way, one agenda, one leader, one set of values, etc. Reducing the wild and wonderful world into one thing that we can grasp, handle, hold onto, and advance.

We do this in movement all the time. I have been in countless meetings where there was a moment of creative abundance and energy, and then someone said we need-ed to pick one thing to get behind, or a three- or five- or ten-point plan. What came next was sometimes very com-pelling and visionary. Other times—often times—it was reductionist, agreeing on the lowest common denomina-tor, the least exciting thing, because that was the only place there was unity. There was often a general sense of dissatis-faction and collective shrugging into this unity that was not invigorating. Authentic, exciting unity takes time, and lots of experimenting.

The other tragedy of this quick narrowing is that people get left out, not just in a slightly hurtful way, but left out of how we construct every aspect of society, infrastructure and culture. We come up with incredible plans that don't account for crucial segments of our communities—I've wit-nessed this as well, unity that entails leaving behind people with disabilities; or trans, Indigenous, immigrant communi-ties, and others.

It isn't that we never need sharp, directed, focused and even single-issue moments—we absolutely do. It's just that we live in a system that thrives when conditions are abundant and di-verse, in a universe that holds contradictions and multitudes, and we often reject that chaotic fertile reality too soon, as if we can't tolerate the scale of our own collective brilliance.

In my observations of the natural world, there are exam-ples of scale that offer another way—when we think about snowflakes, grains of sand, waves in water, stars—there is ev-idence that many possibilities exist for how we manifest in-side our potential. Then there are wavicles—entities that are simultaneously waves and particles. Then there is quantum mechanics, which examines the smallest units of our universe and shows that everything we think of as solid and singular is actually fluid and multitudes.

Excerpt from "Notes Toward a Theory of Quantum Blackness"[5]

By Sofia Samatar

2. Infinities

Blackness cannot be integrated with quantum mechanics at very high energies. At lower energies, it is ignored; to address energies at or higher than the Planck scale, a new theory of quantum Blackness is required.

To address vulnerability. To address a relationship to interruption. To integrate the vibration of urban backyards.

Blackness has been described as nonrenormalizable. Its behavior depends on an infinite number of independent parameters. Therefore, to develop a consistent theory of quantum Blackness one must conduct an infinite number of experiments.

The experiment of zones. Analysis of prison-flesh attraction. The experiment of the "Black smile." Of the child.

Infinite kinship experiments. Infinite gestures.

A laboratory vast enough to contain the wall.

Sometimes we were so tired we couldn't lie down. We would take walks. We would buy nothings. We joked about the experiment of the corner store. The experiment of the fiercely freezing, neon-colored drinks. Of the red powder on the fingers. Fluorescent light.

---

5   Sofia Samatar, "Notes Toward a Theory of Quantum Blackness," *Strange Horizons* 29 (February 29, 2016); with respect to the work of Black Quantum Futurism, http://blackquantumfuturism.tumblr.com/, reprinted with permission.

Take into consideration the presence of a curved background.

Consider imaginary time.Noncommunicative geometry. The "trapped surface."

Consider the implications of the phrase: "cannot be integrated."

Consider string theory, which introduced the concept of vibration.

Experiments in exhaustion. Consider that the problem of quantum Blackness will mean different things to different researchers. My colleague died of complications from a condition called "hood disease," but she herself always referred to it as "white supremacy disease."

It is possible that the Black force particle does not exist: that the effects we observe derive from a different mechanism.

As my colleague wrote before her untimely death: Only two words in this research have meaning, and they are not [Quantum] [Blackness]

At the human scale, in order to create a world that works for more people, for more life, we have to collaborate on the process of dreaming and visioning and implementing that world. We have to recognize that a multitude of realities have, do, and will exist.

Collaborative Ideation is a way to get into this—ideation is the process of birthing new ideas, and the practice of collaborative ideation is about sharing that process as early as possible. This is not to say there is no space for individual creation—I love the selfishness of closing the world out and unleashing the realm of my imagination and creativity. But how do we disrupt the constant individualism of creation when it comes to society, our shared planet, our resources?

The more people who cocreate the future, the more people whose concerns will be addressed from the foundational level in this world.

Meaningful collaboration both relies on and deepens relationship—the stronger the bond between the people or groups in collaboration, the more possibility you can hold. In beginning this work, notice who you feel drawn to, and where you find ease. And notice who challenges you, who makes the edges of your ideas grow or fortify. I find that my best work has happened during my most challenging collaborations, because there are actual differences that are converging and creating more space, ways forward that serve more than one worldview.

"As a part of our liberation, the Earth teaches us that everything—E-V-E-R-Y-T-H-I-N-G—is connected. The soil needs rain, organic matter, air, worms and life in order to do what it needs to do to give and receive life. Each element is an essential component.

"Organizing takes humility and selflessness and patience and rhythm while our ultimate goal of liberation will take many expert components. Some of us build and fight for land, healthy bodies, healthy relationships, clean air, water, homes, safety, dignity, and humanizing education. Others of us fight for food and political prisoners and abolition and environmental justice. Our work is intersectional and multifaceted. Nature teaches us that our work has to be nuanced and steadfast. And more than anything, that we need each other—at our highest natural glory—in order to get free."
—Dara Cooper

That is how *Octavia's Brood* came to exist, because Walidah and I have radically different visions and work styles—Walidah pays attention to values-alignment in every detail. I skim, focused on patterns and magic.

I've worked with Invincible Ill Weaver over many years and we identified early that where they are gloriously thorough, I am fast and efficient. Where they seek research, how things happened in the past and lessons to apply forward—building a case—I feel things, mostly finding my attention on the present and future.

Projects with both of these collaborators have been able to accommodate tons of perspectives and mobilized lots of other creative work, in part because of the space between the collaborators at the core, and learning to communicate and ideate within that space.

Occupy and Black Lives Matter are two large-scale recent efforts that take this collaborative ideation to a movement level, proliferating futures from a place of possibility, of multitudinous paths forward towards a shared dream.

In our work for *Octavia's Brood*, Walidah and I articulated that "all organizing is science fiction," by which we mean that social justice work is about creating systems of justice and equity in the future, creating conditions that we have never experienced. That is a futurist focus, and the practices of collaboration and adaptation and transformative justice, are science fictional behavior. We didn't create this understanding, we observed it amongst the afrofuturists and sci fi writers and creators we grew up loving and being liberated by. Language changes with time, and sometimes the word for a people or an action comes centuries late. But I want to always remember and honor those who stayed and stay future oriented in the face of oppression.

> "There is nothing new under the sun, but there are new suns."
> —Octavia Butler, *Parable of the Trickster*[6]

6   This quote was shared by Gerry Canavan, the first researcher to go through the unpublished drafts of *The Parable of the Trickster* in the Huntington papers, via https://lareviewofbooks.org/article/theres-nothing-new-sun-new-suns-recovering-octavia-e-butlers-lost-parables#!

Afrofuturism and #Blackspring[7]

We tend to think and speak of afrofuturism as the far off future, something beyond our current comprehension and planet. But now is the only moment. And we hope things will be different in the next now. And I must admit, I am excited about the near future.

What are we about to do after this winter of discontent?

We say, Black lives matter!

An afrofuturist assertion.

Because we see something other than the normative truths of this place...we see something that is not here...

We see the future, cast over this devastating present moment.

We see,

And we believe.

We know,

And we bend the world to assert and embody that Black lives matter.

That, to me, is the heart of afrofuturism, as I choose to understand it.[8] Labels don't excite me so much, but concepts turn me on. The concept of seeing and creating the future from a perspective that has the lineage of an African seed, of something older and other than western, feels healing to me.

We, of that displaced diasporic seed, who involuntarily reach back to the motherland in our dreams, have been scattered so far from each other.

And in spite of all the odds, we have been resilient.

I cannot speak emotionally about the journeys of the other seed clusters, though I am seeking stories all the time,

---

7   These are notes from my keynote speech at the Afrofuturism Conference, New School, New York City, 2015.

8   In his essay "Black to the Future," Mark Dery defined Afrofuturism as "speculative fiction that treats African-American themes and addresses African-American concerns in the context of 20th century technoculture." Read the essay at https://thenewblack5324.files .wordpress.com/2012/08/mark-dery-black-to-the-future.pdf.

reading Nnedi Okorafor and Ben Okri and Credo Mutwa and wanting to know more.

Lately I've been obsessing over the afrofuturism and justice orientation of slave-era Blacks, because our situation today feels so terrifying, and exhausting and sometimes hopeless, and there's so much trauma and grief to bear, and yet we survived that.

Not individually, but collectively.

Not all of those Black people were afrofuturists, but to focus on afrofuturists in the Black social-justice tradition, I would note that:

Africans leaping off of slaver ships were afrofuturists.

Slave-era parents teaching their babies a foreign alphabet in the candlelit dirt were afrofuturists.

Black women dissociating themselves through to tomorrow while being raped into motherhood were afrofuturists.

Those who raised the children of violence, and those who chose not to, all were predicting the future and articulating their choices.

Slaves who ran to freedom, and slaves who ran to their deaths, were afrofuturists.

It is the emphasis on a tomorrow that centers the dignity of that seed, particularly in the face of extinction, that marks, for me, the afrofuturist.

And of course there are the big ones, whose names have made it through the erasers of history books, into our mouths—Harriet, Sojourner, Frederick, John, Malcolm, James, Ella, Martin, Nina, June, Toni.

Octavia.

Now it is our work, and the exciting thing about this time is that we are learning to name ourselves, our distinctions and solidarities. Our afrofuturisms. Developing enough of a common dream language that we can be that much more explicit about the real futures we are shaping into existence.

We are touching the future, reaching out across boundaries and post-apocalyptic conditions to touch each other, to call each other out as family, as beloveds. "All that you touch, you change. All that you change, changes you."[9] we are making ourselves vulnerable enough to be changed, which will of course change what Black existence means. Octavia Butler, who gave us that philosophical spirit poem "Earthseed" that I just quoted, is a bridge for many of us, between this world, and the narratives that pull us through to the next realm, or the parallel universe, or the future in which we are the protagonists.

We are creating a world we have never seen. We are whispering it to each other cuddled in the dark, and we are screaming it at people who are so scared of it that they dress themselves in war regalia to turn and face us.

Because of our ancestors, because of us, and because of the children we are raising, there will be a future without police and prisons. Yes.

There will be a future without rape. Without harassment, and constant fear, and childhood sexual assault.

A future without war, hunger, violence. With abundance.

Where gender is a joyful spectrum. Where my nephew would not be bullied for his brilliant differentness. Where each of our bodies is treated like sacred ground, whether we have insurance or not.

Visionary fiction (a term that Walidah coined) includes sci fi, speculative fiction, fantasy, magical realism, myth, all of it. In addition to this intentional genrecide, visionary fiction intentionally explores how change happens from the bottom up,

How change works in collective ways, disrupting the single white male hero narrative,

Centering marginalized communities... Meaning we are the center of the story, as opposed to the sexy and unbelievably stylish sidekick. And visionary fiction is hard, and realistic, and hopeful. It's neither utopian nor dystopian, it's more like life.

Imagination is one of the spoils of colonization, which in many ways is claiming who gets to imagine the future for a given geography. Losing our imagination is a symptom of

---

9   Butler, *Parable of the Sower*.

trauma. Reclaiming the right to dream the future, strengthening the muscle to imagine together as Black people, is a revolutionary decolonizing activity.

Some of the key practices that show up in Octavia Butler's work are collaboration, compassion, curiosity, romantic and sensual and non-possessive love, play, mediation, and the patience that comes from seeing ourselves in a much longer arc of time than we are encouraged to see in the instantaneous culture of the modern world.

What we are all really asking—what Octavia was asking— is how do we, who know the world needs to change, begin to practice being different? How do we have to be for justice to truly be transformative? Not them, that massive amorphous "them" that is also us, in our heads and hearts, or that loves us, or that is tired of this shit but is family to us… Not them, because maybe they don't recognize yet that these changes are the key to human survival. But *us*, us who are awake and awakening. How do we need to be for Black lives to matter? What do we need to heal in ourselves in order to offer a future of any real peace? Or to become the protagonists of this human story—and earn the flip of the page of all the sentient life in the universe? To claim the future as a compelling place for our miracles?

This is everything.

Science fiction is not fluffy stuff. Afrofuturism is not just the coolest look that ever existed. The future is not an escapist place to occupy. All of it is the inevitable result of what we do today, and the more we take it in our hands, imagine it as a place of justice and pleasure, the more the future knows we want it, and that we aren't letting go.

> "Nature also teaches me persistence and perseverance, because in the end 'nothing stops nature.' If a rose can grow out of the concrete, then so can we."
> —Micah Hobbes Frazier

"I love bio-mimicry as a concept of human society learning from nature to make our lives better. In progressive arguments, we often point to examples in nature to prove our point. What's ironic is that the left often discounts religion, but what makes the "it happens in nature" argument so powerful is this belief that nature is created by some higher being or a force beyond us. I think that is my attraction to nature. Its somehow proof of faith. Something more powerful than us yet that we are apart of at the same time. The most powerful thing for organizers to have, I believe, is faith. This belief that we can win, that we can change the world, that we can all be better."

—Terry Marshall

CONVERSATIONS

I met Grace Lee Boggs when she was ninety-two, and slowly grew a friendship with her, a friendship imbued with the mentorship that happens across a sixty-three-year age gap. We mostly built our friendship in her living room, but I also got to attend a Beloved Community gathering with her and Shea Howell, which remains to me of one of the most incredible and intimate experiences I have ever had with other humans. Grace was difficult, exacting, funny, furious, curious, and believed in her right to assert her ideas, her critiques, her visions in the world.

Grace had core questions, questions she asked for decades, of everyone she met. And she had many answers to these questions, and with her eyes and her attention she would offer her judgment on how people answered these questions. And she kept asking. She would watch all of us grow as we answered her questions again and again.

One of her core questions was, "What time is it on the clock of the world?" My answer to that question has become, "Time to close the gap between vision and practice. Time for those of us who seek justice and liberation to BE just and liberated, to be of this place fully."

Emergent strategy is my answer to Grace.

One of the biggest lessons I learned from Grace in the years I spent sitting in her living room, reading her work, bringing loved ones to meet her (including my parents, whom she wrapped around her finger), and singing to her, is that conversation is a crucial way to explore what we believe and to make new understandings and ideas possible.

In my ideal world, we would sit down together and talk through all of these things. Instead I am going to share a series of conversations that I had in the course of creating this book, conversations with people whose work and ways of being excite me. I hope you can weave yourself into these conversations, which bring the various elements into the complex space of the human experience.

"I love trees. big ass trees. trees weather all storms cuz they're rooted.

my organizing needs to be rooted. rooted in my principles, rooted in the love for the people, rooted in community and a vision that extends to the skies like big ass redwoods."
—Hiram Rivera

"Our fruits are only as strong as our roots."
—Thenjiwe Tameika McHarris

A Conversation on Consensus with Autumn Meghan Brown[1]

adrienne: *Would you describe yourself as an emergent strategist?*

Autumn: Definitely. Over time, as I have learned about this approach (through your workshops and through experimenting), I have recognized that it feels not only aligned with my theory of change, but also that emergence has its own momentum, which means that it happens anyway regardless of how structured I attempt to be.

adrienne: *Beautiful. I think consensus is a beautiful way to be in emergent practice together. Could you share a bit about how you approach consensus?*

Autumn: I think part of my approach to consensus is that I recognize it as our normal human orientation. We are innately cooperative and social beings. I often tell my students that there is a reason humans are born unable to move, dress, eat on their own, unable to protect themselves. We are born into relationships of dependence and interdependence. It's what we long for, and we struggle within decision-making models and structures that don't support that deepest desire. So part of my approach to teaching consensus, over time, has been to ground it historically. Cause I'm also a history nerd, so that's how I get my nerd out.

adrienne: *Right. That is so important, to counter our socialization.*

---

1   Autumn is a member of the Anti-Oppression Resource and Training Alliance (AORTA), and is a consensus trainer and facilitator whose movement roles have included Interim Executive Director at RECLAIM, founding member of Rock Dove Collective, and Board Member of Common Fire. She is a mother, theologian, writer, artist, and also one of my sisters.

Autumn: I share how differently consensus arises within culture vs. political/movement spaces, and the history of consensus practice in movement spaces as deeply related to feminist and Indigenous movement work. That it is work of collective liberation, no matter how often it is co-opted.

And then I make people practice and experiment with it, so they understand it as a practice that requires time to build skill, to drop into a different sense of time and space. For me, approaching consensus is very much about: Do we have the tools? Are we willing to fuck up?

adrienne: *Cause people generally feel it's too hard?*

Autumn: They do. And part of that is because they want it to be an antidote to power. And it's not. So that would be the other core aspect of my approach: recognizing that consensus does not mean or require equal status. It rather requires equal voice. But truly, it is also hard because our society functions less and less along the lines of what we need, as humans, to make good decisions.

adrienne: *How is equal voice possible without equal status (asking for a friend)?*

Autumn: Good question… I think it's possible when there is transparency, and when an understanding of status is grounded in a framework of systemic and institutional oppression. Folks need to understand that status or rank is both not accidental but also not individual, not in the way that we are socialized to think status is. When we are in the space of collectivity, we have to reckon with what we are consenting to and not consenting to. Once we get to that space, we see some forms of status fall away as people realize they don't have to consent to it. And then we see some forms of status remain as folks realize it's not a threat. When we can stand in knowing another person's power without feeling threatened, that can be powerful in itself. I love that part of consensus actually. Being able to really see another person's expertise without being upset by it.

adrienne: *That feels so important!! Like—everyone isn't the same. But everyone is valuable.*

Autumn: Exactly! And I can really let go and let other people hold their expertise, and I can call it forward and learn. And that is healthy for a group. A group that is always making decisions isn't a group that is always learning, necessarily, but learning is an essential function of making good decisions. And in order to learn together you have to be good at humility and curiosity.

adrienne: *Does consensus happen in nature?*

Autumn: Oooh that is an awesome question…That I don't know the answer to… But I would imagine that a lot of sympathetic relationships between different species requires consensus because they require consent—"watering hole" consent. Like after a drought we all need to drink. So we can't be focused on eating each other in daylight. Let that be for the darkness.

adrienne: *That's beautiful.*

Autumn: Certainly you see a lot of mammalian communities where consensus is operative. Bonobos, meerkats…

adrienne: *I also think consensus is like water. Many paths, but the future is the ocean. Like we can resist, but it is inevitable, we will have to get together eventually.*

Autumn: It's where we are going, and not all of us will get there. Lol, my dystopic brain.

adrienne: *Well, that's also true. I keep pushing away from utopia. In nature it's more like we all get our day, our time. Nothing blooms 365 days of the year, someone told me that.*

Autumn: Yep. Oof. So real. And our gifts thrive in very different circumstances. I was thinking about that with my singing, like all of the times I have sung in public in the last few years have been by invitation; that I am not as likely to do it if there isn't a specific request. So I have a gift that thrives only upon request.

adrienne: *I love that. I only sing when shamed into it. Or as a joke song. Hmmm. I have other gifts!*

Autumn: Isn't it funny? And we have really beautiful voices.

adrienne: *We really do.*

Autumn: But there are too many things that capture our attention.

adrienne: *Yes! Anything else you want to share about how nature has shaped your facilitation? Or about AORTA!?[2]*

Autumn: AORTA uses some awesome nature-based metaphors for working with systemic oppression. They have this whole thing they do around giant hogweed. I'm still learning it so don't feel equipped to talk about it yet. I tend not to use nature metaphors, but that is because I tend to think of humans as a part of nature, and so I focus more on what is naturally occurring in our relationships. That's not to say that nature doesn't influence my work at all; just to say that it's not my go to. I tend to go to human family as example.

---

2   AORTA is a worker-owned cooperative devoted to strengthening movements for social justice and a solidarity economy. http://aorta .coop/.

Oh one thing—I think living with access to a big natural environment has completely shifted my approach to facilitation. Because I live in the woods and get this front-row seat to the dance of life and death and the big cycles and the way in which a lack of protection and relationship exposes us to danger. It also means I am more likely to go to breath. It means I am more likely to go slow and let things take up space where I used to rush. Living in the woods is teaching me to notice more. Because I can see how everything's survival is related to how it's tuned into the space it occupies, its ability to notice, to be noticed.

adrienne: *Hey one more thing—are you the reason Occupy knew how to use consensus?*

Autumn: Lol, I'm not the only reason. In fact, one of the folks I worked closely with to build the consensus curriculum that I taught for years, David Graeber, was on the ground at the beginning of Occupy, and I'm sure he had a lot to do with it. But I trained hundreds of those organizers in consensus over the years preceding Occupy, so I think of it as having a hand in preparing the way for that to happen. Like, Occupy wouldn't have been as successful and wouldn't have had that long-term multiplier effect across the country, if they hadn't been skilled and successful in using consensus, and they were because I trained them up. Does that make sense? And then I know my consensus tools were being used by other folks around the country who were creating Occupy spaces too.

adrienne: *Ok thanks for this—I feel so proud of this and brag on it but realized I hadn't actually asked you the deal, and you're humble about it :) love!*

A Virtuous Cycle with Jodie Tonita[3]

adrienne: *What was the impetus for Social Transformation Project coming into existence? And has that changed with time?*

Jodie: We came into existence to help build a more powerful and effective progressive movement. Our work strengthens the movement's capacity for collaborative action. Initially we invested in leadership development and sharing methodology and tools that make transformational leadership and organizational change practices more accessible. Building on that foundation, our work is now focused on building functional self-organizing networks of progressive leaders who can think together, align around a common agenda, and act together to secure and sustain long-term social change.

adrienne: *Who do you work with?*

Jodie: We partner with leaders who are committed to building trust, cross-movement collaboration, and systemic change. At the heart of the growing network are twenty-two powerful movement leaders from across issue areas that have far-reaching influence and lead critical progressive institutions.[4] Since 2010, we have supported them to connect deeply, build trust, strategize, experiment, and collaborate in ways that build power and unite progressive voices. We know that to reach our shared goals we must grow and evolve the network. To expand, we will draw from the leaders' own

---

3   Jodie Tonita is one of my woes and teachers and friends. Born and raised in Canada, Jodie moved to the US to co-found and executive direct a movement support and strategy effort called the Social Transformation Project (STP), and because she felt the US was a critical place to invest organizing energy.

4   Some of the groups STP works with: National Domestic Workers' Alliance, NARAL, Forward Together, MoveOn.org, Right to the City Alliance, Service Employees International Union and many more.

networks, as well as our trusted relationships with the 500+ leaders of the Rockwood LIO National, Cross-Movement, and the Art of Transformational Consulting alumni networks that we connect and convene.

adrienne: *How have you decided what to do in the world?*

Jodie: When artful leaders have space and support to connect deeply and are challenged to strategize and work together in new ways, possibilities light up at the intersections. We create conditions for this kind of connection, challenge leaders to strategize in new ways and support the emergent ideas and collaborations that arise.

adrienne: *And when do you make adjustments?*

Jodie: We're supporting leaders to experiment with new ways of taking action together, and that requires continuous real-time adjustment. We're using a structured process to systematically track and evaluate their real-world experiments. We're aiming to create a virtuous cycle of aligning, acting, and learning that results in better ideas, strategies, and ways of working that increase our impact.

adrienne: *What have you learned that feels important for movement leaders and participants to hear?*

Jodie: Movement moments are emergent, but there are systemic ways to cultivate networks and collective capacity to strategize and act together in nimble and powerful ways when those moments arise. Leadership development is an important and strategic way to build relationships and trust while equipping leaders with the skills and practices to increase their impact and sustain themselves over the long haul.

Leaders across movements acknowledge that our strategies and ideas are still insufficient and our siloed efforts do not add up to more than the sum of their parts. Our approach to change is too often reactive and haphazard. We are not leveraging knowledge and innovation from other sectors nearly enough. The structures of our organizations, campaigns, and coalitions don't support the kind of experimentation, coordination, and collaboration we need.

Our most promising leaders know all of this to be true and are finding the way, but they struggle to break out of old patterns. They lack the dedicated time, resources, and expertise to invent new systems and structures, and to practice in new ways. Without an engaged and self-organizing network to support their efforts, each leader is left to work alone within the constraints and limits of their own organization's resources and capacities.

Leadership development programs like BOLD, Forward Stance, generative somatics, Move to End Violence, and Rockwood are bringing leaders together across organizations and movements to seed the kinds of networks these leaders need. These programs cultivate leaders who are emotionally resilient and connected to high-trust networks that can act quickly with efficacy and integrity. Many of today's most promising movement-building projects are emerging from these efforts.

We're committed to growing the capacity of these high-trust networks. We want to see them evolve and develop into functional self-organizing networks that can deepen their shared analysis to fuel strategic action, align around long-term priorities, and experiment with collaborative action, learn, and improve their practice. We believe this is the way to build lasting power and make long-term structural change for a more just and sustainable world.

adrienne: *You've also maintained an organizing relationship with folks in Canada. What are you learning through that organizing?*

Jodie: In the US, I work with networks that are by design 50 percent folks of color and are led by women of color. In

Canada, the spaces I am in are predominately white, and power is often held by men. I'm finding I have no patience for it. I'm not interested in "convincing" people, who have no motivation and little interest in sharing power, to do so. I am much more interested in contending for power. There is a huge opportunity in Canada to invest in women of color leaders. To support them to build the power of their community organizations, to build a base that can eventually elect them to political office and hold them accountable. My dream is to support the development of a network of women of color leaders who move into positions of power and organize those institutions to work for their communities. I think if we did this well we could take over the country city by city. This strategy is going to make a lot of people uncomfortable. Getting there is going to be turbulent. Developing the capacity to navigate internal and external turbulence will be critical to our success. This is what leadership looks like in this moment.

adrienne: *What's on the other side of that turbulence? Why should people keep trying?*

Jodie: In the face of daunting challenges, we must summon the courage to believe we are the ones we have been waiting for, take risks, and experiment towards solutions. We're being asked to believe in our inherent capacity, step into the unknown, and challenge deeply held assumptions. For most of us, that's radically disruptive and contrary to how we've organized ourselves to succeed in life to date.

If you're reading this book, you're at least considering this path. Why do it? Because you will become the leader we need. Together we will become the leaders we collectively need. And in the process we will continuously grow and shift and change to meet each new challenge.

My colleague Eugene Kim has this great tool called the Strategy / Culture Bicycle. He says that developing an effective strategy and culture is about asking the right questions:

Where are we now? Who are we today? Where do we want to go? Who do we want to become? How do we get there? What I love about this is that where we are going and who we need to be to get there are married. We can't get to a new destination without shifting who and how we are. This is another reason why networks are important. They give us places to come together to see patterns, learn new practices (ways of being), and reach new heights.

adrienne: *How do you ground yourself in this work?*

Jodie: I have a commitment I repeat to myself in key leadership moments throughout the day. "I trust myself in the face of the unknown." While I say it, I focus on my breath, ground through my heels, feel my back, and remember that all of my skills and experience are available and have prepared me for just this moment. I have my woes, who know what I am aiming for, are tracking my situation, and will support and challenge me. Having peers who share the work of becoming the ones we have been waiting for is essential. And when things get turbulent I reach out for specific supports like acupuncture, therapy, and somatic bodywork.

Basically for Being a Human Being: Meditation with Dani McClain[5]

adrienne: *When did you begin meditating?*

Dani: I was introduced to formal meditation practice in 2004 or 2005 in Cincinnati—I started going to this little dharma center. I had never sat before—like on a cushion or chair— and have someone tell me to focus on my breath and identify

---

5   Dani McClain writes and reports on race, reproductive health, policy, and politics. She is a contributing writer at the *Nation*, and a fellow at the Nation Institute. She is also a new mom and one of my woes.

thoughts and let them go and give me formal mindfulness training. So that was my introduction. I got away from it for a while, I didn't have a daily practice. I stopped until I moved to Oakland and someone told me about EBMC [East Bay Meditation Center] and I started going to their Thursday night people of color sits. Spring Washam hosted—she was the first person I would consider my teacher; she introduced me to Buddhism, not just mindfulness. This was '09—my practice began to deepen. In Cincinnati the sangha was very white and older, in Oakland it felt like people my age, and I related to Spring as a Black woman.

One thing that has always struck me was…this was my formal introduction. I have words for sitting, mindfulness, and meditation. But I remember—my grandmother died when I was seven, and I fully remember going on errands with her and she would close her eyes while we were waiting and I would say "Gram, why are you sleeping?" and she would say, "I'm not sleeping, I am resting my eyes." I think many people meditate—they might not call it that or see it as such. But most of us have a way of opening up to what's happening around us, turning inward, not engaging in every stimulus. Not everyone calls it meditation and that's fine.

adrienne: *I think for me so much of it is about landing in now. Stress behind, anxiety ahead, how do we put our attention on now, breath on now. What is your practice now?*

Dani: I don't have a daily practice right now. I had a consistent daily practice through a difficult period of my life, for about two years. I had a practice and then went through a breakup, and my aunt…she was sick and then passed away. During the time she was sick and going through treatment, I had a lot of fear and anticipatory grief—a term I didn't even know yet but I have learned is quite common—when you fear someone might pass away.

I try to go on retreat twice a year, silent retreat. So I would go on retreat, go to EBMC. Then I did this year-long weekly program called "Commit to Dharma," led by Larry Yang, someone I consider a key teacher. During that period, 2012–2015, I was very committed to a sitting practice. And I needed it to stay tethered to some semblance of being able to find joy, being able to function effectively, to take care of my life.

During the course of that practice, in 2014, it was incredible to have a community to practice with, and the sessions, and reflections with teachers. It's not just mindfulness; it's also learning about Buddhist philosophy. Learning what are called the heart practices—"lovingkindness, compassion, joy and equanimity"—was a focus of the class.

They say one way to think about the dharma is that they are two wings of a bird. One wing is the wisdom practices, the other wing is the heart practices. I think of the wisdom practices as being present in the moment, identifying my thoughts and letting them flow away. The focus is on the mind.

But the heart practices are all about the heart. When I sit, I can sit and do a lovingkindness or compassion practice. But meditation is a lot more about the mind. The heart practices are a lot more about the world around you. You practice compassion related to other people around you. In my aunt's final weeks, I was practicing compassion, joy—trying to find moments of sympathetic joy in a difficult situation.

This past year of my life I have had a lot of changes and have been trying to find equanimity. So more recently I don't have a daily sitting practice, but I am much more engaged in the world around me. And I am trying to consciously bring those practices into everything I do.

I would like to get back to a seated daily practice, because I think that is the foundation. But in the absence of that, a rooting in Buddhist principles and philosophy is helpful; it shows up even when I am not on the cushion.

adrienne: *Build a bridge for me between meditation and nature. (Humans dropping into our nature, etc.) Have these practices played into your life as you create life?*

Dani: I grew up in a rural environment. When I think of being a child I think about riding a bike, running all over the place, playing in the woods, fishing with my neighbor. Because of where I grew up, I am really drawn to forests, to sitting in natural places. Gives me a sense of calm. It's easier for me to clear my mind. One reason I like to go on retreat is that they tend to be in these beautiful places, and if you aren't in retreat you can go on long walks. Last year, I went on retreat in Joshua Tree and it was incredible to meditate in the desert—see jackrabbits, these huge black crows, the cactus—to feel like the natural world was my partner in my work, my mindfulness. My practice deepened in California. I have gone on retreat more often at Spirit Rock—the hills of northern California. It's interesting that California has been where I have had the experiences of turning inward—not the environments I am from. But it's nice to get away from traffic sounds, from lights so you can see the night sky, to smell the air free of fumes. The quiet on retreat is hard to come by where I live.

My experience being pregnant: acceptance. The four noble truths—there is suffering. Clinging is the cause of suffering. There is an end to suffering. There is a way out—the noble eightfold path. My pregnancy is a process of letting go... Clinging to anything, to fixed ideas of how things should be, how things are supposed to go, doesn't work. I have had other lessons that showed me that, but this is a really focused way to learn. To be ok with uncertainty, not knowing anything, not knowing what the next day will be like, or next few months, the process of birth, what this person will be like, what their arrival on this plane will be like. There have been times when I am moving through uncertainty in the past few years, where my practice has helped me be ok with that, to not feel like I deserve to know, that none of us are promised that clarity. You're not all that in charge.

adrienne: *Do you feel meditation and mindfulness is important for people working to create change in the world?*

Dani: If this is your life's work then yes, at some point, establishing some practice that helps you connect with yourself and center yourself is vital. Yes. For me it's meditation and Buddhist teachings. I wasn't raised super Christian but I grew up going to Sunday school, bible camp, things like that. I still go to church sometimes. There's something about prayer to me that is more devotional—you have to use your brain more. You have to think it through, be in conversation with god, it's wordy. But there is something in prayer and song that accomplishes what the heart practices do for me. What is important is to have something that brings me back to myself in the midst of a bunch of feelings, opinions, attitudes—in social-change work you are constantly exposed to other people's ways of doing things. I am very sensitive to other people's energies. It's very helpful to get away from that. I touch into what I think, what I feel. To understand that our minds are not real, that we are often projecting things that are not real. The practice helps me differentiate between foolishness, noise, things that are not me. Yes for social-change work—and basically for being a human being.

Finding a community of people to learn from—a teacher, people committed to practice—is really important. I had been curious about this, and what I had done was read books. That isn't the same—you can learn all the concepts, but if you're not practicing it's not the same. Finding a community, a *sangha*, is really, really important. One resource is dharmaseed.org—it's a library of talks, guided meditations. It's something I think about a lot, having moved back to Cincinnati. There's still the dharma center where I learned mindfulness, but I feel so grateful to have spent time in Oakland. There is something really special happening there—teachers doing brilliant work around why Buddhism in the west is so white, and asking what to do about that, in terms of the teaching core, and making (welcoming) more diverse spaces, different sexual orientations, and gender identities. That's so important. If you live in a place like the Bay, NY, DC—you are lucky. You can find a *sangha* that is more like what this country looks like. If you don't—let's figure something out. Finding a practice community you feel connected to is crucial.

ASSESS YOURSELF:

your emergent strategy journal

You can use the following assessment in a few ways:

If you are reading and working through this book as an individual, use these questions for journaling (having a conversation with yourself) and personal assessment. Journal over the course of a few days, rereading your thoughts to feel for alignment in the body (the body never lies).

If you are reading and working through this book in a group, try starting with individual journaling and then have conversations around the answers, asking yourselves where there is alignment to move forward.

You can also use these reflections as a jumping off point, creating a baseline[1] to return to after you have read the book and start to play with the tools.

---

1   Thanks to Faster Than 20's Eugene Kim for teaching me this language of measuring theories over time.

Assessment Quickie

Here is a quick tool for measuring your embodiment of emergent strategy at this moment. Feel free to take multiple times to measure growth.

	Yes	No	I don't know
Do you value small scale growth and change?			
Do you adapt easily to new circumstances?			
Are you comfortable with nonlinear growth and transformation?			
Do you experience conflict as a generative force in your life/work?			
Are you in community/ relationship with people who can and do hold you accountable?			
Do you see change as an opportunity?			
Do you see yourself as a part of the natural world?			

Mostly yes: You are an emergent strategist! Teach us how you do it!

Mostly no: Each no is a place to grow!

Mostly I don't know: Let's learn together—get and stay curious.

Assessment of Fractal

o Are you a perfect living realization of your values and beliefs?

o Is your group a perfect living realization of your collective values and beliefs?

o What are you embodying in your daily life? In your work?

o Individual: Interview three people you trust in your extended community to give you feedback about how you show up in the world. Share you purpose/intention with each of them and ask them to hold that as they answer your questions. Sample questions:

  • What is my impact in the world?

  • In three words, what am I embodying?

  • Where do you think I could grow?

o Organizational:

  • Interview three people in the community your group/organization serves to give you feedback based on how y'all show up in the world. Share with them what you think you are embodying and have a brief discussion on how much you are or are not embodying that.

  • Can everyone in the organization state the vision and mission accurately, even passionately?

Assessment of Adaptation

o **How do I/we respond to positive changes?**
o **How do I/we respond to negative changes?**
o **What is my/our intention?**
o **How do I/we do at keeping my/our intention present during changes?**

With an organization/team/network, have everyone separately rate the group on this scale. Share the ratings and have a discussion on how you made your assessment, and what adaptations are needed.

Our organization/team/network is (choose one)
☐ Too adaptive (we change for anything and lose touch with our purpose/intention).
☐ Highly adaptive and focused.
☐ Pretty adaptive (we could keep relaxing with and into change).
☐ Struggling with adaptation (we get really thrown off our focus/mission when change happens).
☐ Not adaptive (acknowledging reality is the first step).

Assessment of Interdependence and Decentralization

Who do you lean on?

Who leans on you?

(Explore the places where those lists overlap, and where they don't. How can you increase mutual relationship?)

Are all of your needs met? If yes, how? If not, why not?

Did you answer either question above as if it's all your responsibility?

o If not, try it. How does that feel?

o If yes, answer again as if nothing happens with you alone.

Who makes work happen in your group?

☐ Me!

☐ A small core group of us

☐ Everyone shares the work

Does everyone take vacation time and weekends where you work?

Do you feel comfortable using the sick and/or vacation time you earn?

If you disappeared tomorrow (because aliens chose you as the ambassador from Earth to the Alliance of Evolved Planets, for instance), how would your organization respond?

☐ Close its doors

☐ Period of chaos and power struggle

☐ Redistribute my work and be overwhelmed

☐ Redistribute my work and adjust for capacity so that we're still on path

How does your answer to the question above feel?

What could you do to increase decentralized strength in your group?

Assessment of Nonlinear/Iterative

What are you practicing? (Include *anything* you practice/repeat in your life, things you feel positive about, things you feel negative about—from meditation to burn-out, listening to interruption, community accountability to public takedowns, exercise, escaping, etc.)

We spend our lives in unconscious practices, practices that make us deny our true selves, our true power, our collectivism. It takes three hundred repetitions for muscle memory and three thousand repetitions for embodiment.[2] What do you need to practice?

What does your organization/collective/alliance practice? (Include all the things you practice in your collective work—conflict avoidance, glorifying burn-out, over scheduling, mission drifting, check-ins, retreats, active listening, community accountability, etc.)

What do you need to practice?

How long does it take you to understand your feelings and reactions?

How quickly do you (individually, collectively) translate experiences (successes or failures) into lessons?

---

2   This concept is explored in Richard Strozzi-Heckler, *Leadership Dojo* (Berkeley: Frog Books, 2007).

Assessment of Resilience/Transformative Justice

How often do you engage in personal reflection?

How often do you engage in group/movement reflection?

What are your individual resilience practices?

What are resilience practices you and your organization/group/alliance/collective do together?

Do you increase or decrease tension or dramatic moments that happen between you and loved ones (family/lovers/friends)? (If you aren't sure, ask them.)

Do you increase or decrease tension or dramatic moments that happen between you and coworkers/comrades? (If you aren't sure, ask them.)

Does your organization/group increase or decrease tension or dramatic moments that happen between y'all and partner organizations? (If you aren't sure, ask them.)

Do others ask you to mediate, or in other ways support them through conflict?

What is your first reaction to conflict? (Do you address it directly? Avoid it? Get defensive? Turn up? Other?)

How do you feel, and what do you do, when you witness:

Anger?

Joy?

Tears?

Depression?

Imbalanced power dynamics?

Have you or your organization/group ever been involved in a public fight (physical, digital, etc.)? A public takedown? What did you learn from it?

Have you or your group been practicing transformative justice? How could you increase this practice?

Assessment for Creating More Possibility

What are all of your gifts?

Are you living a life that honors all of your gifts?

If yes, how did you create all this possibility for yourself?

If no, how can you create more possibility today? Tomorrow? This month? This year?

What are your organization's unique gifts?

Is your organization able to hold complexity?

SPELLS AND PRACTICES FOR EMERGENT STRATEGY

Emergent Strategy is about shifting the way we see and feel the world and each other. If we begin to understand ourselves as practice ground for transformation, we can transform the world.

I have spoken about practice many times throughout this book, asking in many words: What is it we need to practice as individuals and communities to come more into alignment with the emergent practices of the universe we know as home?

My practices have included meditation, somatics, visionary fiction, facilitation, working out, yoga, intimate community on social media, check ins with woes/buddies, orgasmic meditation, sex, self-documentation (self-love selfies! Learning to see beauty and power in my standard breaking appearance), sugar shifting, sabbatical (big one in 2012, annual mini-sabbaticals since then), poetry, unscheduled time, moon-cycle rituals, tarot (I am such a fan of this practice that I have bought five other people tarot decks), sage and frankincense cleansing of my home, journaling. I love intentional periods of practice, daily practices, new practices, and even outgrowing practices.

I share in this chapter some areas of practices that can unlock the emergent potential we hold. There are also some spells—these are little poems that shift my state of being and power. I offer them to use, and also to encourage you to create spells for your own self-shifting work.

A lot of these practices and spells came to me, or were primarily practiced outside of an organizational context. But I have found that the work of cultivating personal resilience, healing from trauma, self-development and transformation is actually a crucial way to expand what any collective body can be. We heal ourselves, and we heal in relationship, and from that place, simultaneously, we create more space for healed communities, healed movements, healed worlds. What I offer here are the core ways I have tapped into my own power and wholeness, and ways I have supported others to tap into their own wholeness and transformation. And fractal strategy suggests wholeness in our organizers yields wholeness in our future.

I am a fan of being creative and self-directive with practices. What are the practices you need to line your life up with your values and beliefs?

Woes/Coevolution Through Friendship

Did I thank the prolific and joyful Canadian rapper Drake yet for bringing the term "woes" to my attention? Woes stands for "Working On Excellence," and I've reveled in it as a way to note those people in my life with whom I am intentionally growing.

I have sets of woes—people who know my north star, who know my challenges, and who hold me accountable to my own development, celebrating my self-awareness and growth. And it's all mutual. We are in daily contact, and we have intensive visits to check in on our development.

My sisters are one set of my woes, and for a few years now we have instituted a sister check-in during any family visits. Everyone else supports us with childcare and scheduling so that we get the time together to go deep. We each take a turn of sharing what has moved since we were last together, where we need support, and what's coming up that just needs to be shared. Often the biggest support we need is to speak the truth out loud to those who will hold it with us from a vantage point of unconditional love.[1]

It's friendship, but with a lot of transparency and intention woven into it. Another way of speaking about this is *coevolution through friendship*:

Coevolution is "the change of a biological object triggered by the change of a related object."

One of the outcomes of the "Engage Community of Practice" year of building relationship and sharing of ourselves, was an idea articulated toward the end by participant Gibrán Rivera: coevolution through friendship. Meaning: we evolve in relationships of mutual transformation.

Since the community's formal time ended, I have watched and felt this relational coevolution continue in a variety of ways, including close daily personal contact, occasional opportunities for mutual support, noticing and supporting each other's work and growth from afar, and being more intentional about bringing this practice into the way we hold all of our relationships.

---

1   See "Liberated Relationships" in the "Transformative Justice" chapter of this book.

I have been really aware of the power of coevolution through friendship as I have been in what feels like a growth spurt. Babies do this, suddenly overnight become taller, fuller, using new words, more confident in their bodies and complex in their communications. It's pretty incredible to watch—and to feel that the growth doesn't end even if it changes form. In this period, I have been supported, inspired, encouraged, and witnessed by a marvelous circle full of people in their own growth.

The very nature of this is iterative, so I am not writing any definitive guidelines up for y'all. But it is so delicious and impactful that I wanted to share some of what I am noticing, some elements of coevolution through friendship.

Self-transformation.

Both/all people in the relationship and community are committed to their own self-transformation. We see ourselves as microcosms of the world, and work to shift oppressive patterns in our bodies, hearts, minds, speech, interactions, liberating ourselves into purpose, liberating our communities into new practices. We each set the pace of our own transformation.

Curiosity.

We have curiosity about our own lives as learning labs for our values and figuring out what it means to be human at this moment in time. And we have curiosity about each other's lives, about why we do what we do, about the roots of our behaviors. We want to know if there are lessons and changes available in the reflection and action cycle of life. This curiosity ranges from philosophical to academic, historical, nosy, somatic. Our lives are our life's work. What matters is that we are authentic with the questions, that we believe the answers are important, and we listen to each other accordingly.

Vulnerable reflection.

We reach out to each other and say things like "something incredible is happening," "I don't know," "I fucked up," "I think I hurt someone," "I'm overwhelmed," "I'm terrified," "I think I'm hurting," "I'm lost," "Am I falling in/out of love?," "_____ happened, what should I do?," "I want to do something new/different/marvelous/dangerous/that feels essential to my soul—help!," and so on. We ask others to be mirrors for us at our most vulnerable places, so we can see what we are learning, see new possibilities in our lives.

Pattern disrupting.

I know I am always whole theoretically, but I don't always feel that way, I feel half sometimes, I feel fragmented sometimes, messy. Being whole includes owning all of that as me. When I am feeling fragmented or limited, seeing any of my friends in their wholeness reminds me of my own capacity. And as I stand in my wholeness, which includes being more honest with myself and others about what I want and who I am in the world, it exerts a pressure on others, both to receive me and to become more whole in themselves. This disrupts those familiar diminishing patterns in my friends and in myself, the internalization of a world that has rejected every aspect of my identity at some point. Counter rejection. Still I rise. And new patterns become possible, more interconnected and interdependent patterns that rely on being open.

Present and intentional.

This is perhaps the biggest place to practice. Life is not happening to us. We are learning to be in the actual current moment, to recognize where we have choice... In a terrifying twist, it turns out we always have it. So the great question is: how to be intentional, in the present moment, to take responsibility for your state of being, and for your life? Another participant-teacher in the community of practice, Jane Sung E Bai, asked us to consider, "What if I am responsible for everything?" It's not a singular task, to be responsible for what happens in this world—we do not exist or transform in isolation. We are in this universe. We are actively reflecting on how to be in our lives, to best embody our greatness and to yield a more liberated future for ourselves, and thus, in the fractal sense, for all of existence.

There is a lot to be careful of. We are not yet masterful, even though there are moments of collective genius. Sometimes we misread each other, push each other too hard, get defensive, or give unsolicited coevolution pressure.

Sometimes what is happening in the world is so terrifying and urgent that we forget our complexity, or wonder why we would spend time on ourselves or take time for our friendships when there is so much external work to do. What I am noticing is that it is not a privilege to practice coevolution through friendship—it is the deepest work.

I believe it is how communities have survived.

I believe it is Harriet Tubman going back to free others, because it wasn't enough to free only herself.

I believe it is Ubuntu[2] active in my life.

I believe it is the freedom that we are longing for, which will never be given to us, which we have to create, the pulsing life force of the collective body we are birthing, the rhythm of a shared heart.

STOP HATING: A SPELL

let me pull the weed up by the root
and notice the soil that i stand on
is this a necessary vitriol
is *this* what i choose now to rant on?
is there nothing to build
and nothing to grow
no more to offer up
nothing to know

---

2   Ubuntu is a Nguni Bantu concept that translates to "I am because you are"; http://www.ubuntu.thiyagaraaj.com/Home/about-ubuntu/ubuntu -philosophy-meaning#TOC-Archbishop-Desmond-Tutu-further -explained-Ubuntu-in-2008.

is there a way now
that i could let go
can i look in the mirror
and love me more

Authenticity chant:

Let me not posture
Let me not front
Let me not say yes to
Lives I don't want
Let me not use words that don't mean a thing
Let me be fly
as I am, no trying
Let me good
For my heart, not my rep
Let me be still
When I can't take a step
Don't let me get too caught
Creating my face
Let me just love me
All over the place

Visionary Fiction

Art is not neutral. It either upholds or disrupts the status quo, advancing or regressing justice. We are living now inside the imagination of people who thought economic disparity and environmental destruction were acceptable costs for their power. It is our right and responsibility to write ourselves into the future. All organizing is science fiction. If you are shaping the future, you are a futurist. And visionary fiction is a way to practice the future in our minds, alone and together.[3]

---

3   "Visionary fiction" is a term coined by Walidah Imarisha, co-editor of
     Octavia's Brood.

Visionary fiction is neither utopian nor dystopian, instead it is like real life: Hard, realistic… Hopeful as a strategy. Visionary fiction disrupts the hero narrative concept that one person (often one white man, often Matt Damon) alone has the skills to save the world. Cultivate fiction that explores change as a collective, bottom-up process. Fiction that centers those who are currently marginalized—not to be nice, but because those who survive on the margins tend to be the most experientially innovative—practicing survival-based efficiency, doing the most with the least, an important skill area on a planet whose resources are under assault by less marginalized people. Visionary fiction is constantly applying lessons from our past to our future(s).

The best way to practice visionary fiction is to get to writing. The *Octavia's Brood* website offers workshops, and you can also write on your own, form writing groups, and share stories with others.[4] You have worlds inside you. You have permission to share them.

Meditation

My meditation teachers include but are not limited to: Dani McClain; Angel Kyodo Williams; Jesse Maceo Vega-Frey; Thich Naht Hanh; Sam Conway; a spirit named Jai at Kalani; Robert Gass, Spenta Kandawalli, and Chris Lymbertos; Richard Strozzi-Heckler; a stream of yoga teachers; my nibblings and every baby I have every held; and many more.

"My mother was a lifelong activist, and I truly believe that her fight for civil rights—and the traumas she suffered during that fight—cut her life short. So, to me, the ocean represents the importance of self care. My mother loved music, but ultimately I do not believe she had a quiet or steady enough

---

practice to counteract the negativity and anger she built up through her work. Staring at the ocean, or standing with one's feet at the shoreline to feel the vastness of the tide as it pulls away, would be a therapeutic practice for social justice workers—or perhaps even meditating about it, if no ocean is nearby. Life and true change are bigger than all of us. Like Martin, we may not all get "there" (there is no "there"), but we can see it on the horizon. We have to learn to count victories even as we continue to agitate. We cannot become so jaded that we lose joy in everything because the flaws loom too large. The journey is the work, the work is the journey. The ocean's ebbs and flows may remind us of this better than anything."

—Tananarive Due

I resisted meditation for so long. I said it just didn't suit my personality, or that I wasn't down to sit, that I could meditate while doing other things—active non-meditative things.

I was in good company with this, particularly in social justice spaces—everything we are working on is actually urgent—people are being hurt at every level, people and species are dying, the planet is being damaged. We are not making it up. Setting aside time from our work can feel violently selfish.

And yet! If we haven't cultivated mindfulness in our attention, how do we ever expect to break out of the cycle of crisis response? How will we ever put our attention onto solutions, put our attention onto the new practices we need?

Meditation kept waiting for me, around every corner, in every room. Grief was the gift that finally let me understand meditation.

In teaching basic meditation at my Windcall Retreat, Black Zen teacher Angel Kyodo Williams once said that our access to the global scale of suffering has become immediate, through technology, but we have not developed the capacity to be with that increased awareness of suffering.[5] I have felt the truth of this many times in my life, particularly as loved ones have transitioned beyond this life, and as I have been politicized, awakened to the specific and overwhelming suffering that is funded by US tax dollars. I have felt my small hands up against these giants of death, of imperialism, of my own hopelessness.

What my meditation teachers have shared with me is that meditation is about choosing where my attention goes. Training my attention. And that when I am overcome by sadness, loss, anger, joy, desire, restlessness, or other emotions, it helps to be able to drop into myself and choose—to be with the emotions intentionally, to listen for what is needed. This has been a path into emergent strategy—the more I listen, the more I understand the interconnectedness of the world, and my place in it, my insignificance, my wholeness, our collective potential and beauty.

There are many many many methods for meditation. I am going to share a few tips that have made meditation possible for me, and that bring me into deeper awareness of emergence.

1. Breath and sensation awareness is the foundational entry into meditation that works for me. Just noticing the breath coming in and out of my body, in through the nose, out through the mouth. Both the idea of the breath, visualizing nourishing breath moving through the body, and the sensations of the breath, the movement of the chest and abdomen, the air against the upper lip, moving through the mouth.

Bringing the attention back to the breath no matter how often or where it wanders.

Ursula Le Guin speaks to this: "To sit and be fully aware of the air going in and out of your nose, and nothing else,

---

5   Windcall is an incredible retreat for activists and organizers. To learn more or apply to attend, see www.windcall.org.

this sounds really stupid. If you haven't tried it yet, try it. It is really stupid. Nothing your intellect can do to help you do it. This must be why so many people for so long have used it as a way towards wisdom."[6]

2. Reading the work of Thich Nhat Hanh and Pema Chodron has been helpful when relating to thoughts during meditation. I used to think I was supposed to be NOT thinking, and then I learned that many people who meditate, even those who have done it for years and do long silent retreats and stuff, are actually in the tug of war between thinking and being the whole time. Being aware that one is thinking, noticing when thought is happening, can be liberating. The content of the thoughts becomes less important, it is the choice to be thinking vs. breathing.

3. I have actually found the shivasana position in yoga is best for my body for meditation—laying flat on my back, palms up, sinking into the floor or bed. After years of trying to meditate sitting up and spending the entire time in pain, I noticed that the times I felt most capable of meditation were at the end of yoga classes. When I share this with people they always ask, "but don't you fall asleep?" I usually meditate in the morning, so I am already rested, but at night I will return to this often and meditate until I fall asleep. And it seems to be good for my quality of sleep and my dream life to head into sleep in a meditative state.

4. Silence is nice for meditation, but rare in my life. I like to make soundtracks for my meditations, energies moving up or down according to what I am seeking in the meditation. I have also recently gotten into guided meditations[7]—especially those that cultivate lovingkindness, or metta meditation[8]

---

6   Ursula Le Guin, *The Wave in the Mind: Talks and Essays on the Writer, the Reader, and the Imagination* (Shambala, 2004).

7   Using "Insight" meditation app.

8   Metta meditation is a very simple ritual of developing lovingkindness towards yourself and the whole world. As you meditate you say, to yourself or aloud, "May I be happy, may I be healthy, may I be free

5. Use poetry! In our generative somatics courses, we often read poems at the beginning and end of our meditations. Some of my favorites for meditation are:

"The Prison Cell," Mahmoud Darwish;

"The Journey," Mary Oliver;

"Yes, We Can Talk," Mark Nepo;

and everything from June Jordan, Adrienne Rich, Warsan Shire, or Nayirrah Waheed.

6. Time the meditation! My woe Dani has been a gentle teacher and inspiration on my meditation path. One tool she offered me is the "Insight" meditation app, which I use on my phone. Timed meditation is a must for me, and the app marks beginning, end and interim time with bells. This allows me to relax into the meditation, not opening my eyes and looking at the clock desperately every thirty seconds.

I had to start very small, setting the timer for three minutes, which felt like forever. I have built up to a regular practice of forty-five minutes, with my longest continuous meditation at a hundred minutes the night that my mentor Grace transitioned. I consider my meditation practice foundational—I may add or subtract other practices based on what I need to focus on in a given moment, but meditation is a daily practice.

Somatics

"The dream of the cell is to become two. The evolutionary thrust surges through us as dreams, sensations, longings, images, and inexplicable utterances and gestures. We are constantly adapting, creating, filling, emptying as we become the dream. From the elegant simplicity of our cells

from harm and suffering." And then you repeat it for someone you love, someone you feel aversion to, and then for the whole world.

to the vast complex networks of our brain we are
becoming more.

"In aikido we surrender to the spiral that lives
in the blood and plasma of our veins, to our
circulating breath, to our turning dance in gravity,
to the galactic revolutions that spin in the heav-
ens. Spirals that rise and fall as do civilizations,
tectonic plates, to our standing and lying down
every day."
—Richard Strozzi-Heckler

Somatics is the study of the *soma*, a Greek word that means
"the living organism in its wholeness." It is a methodology for
transformation that helps us understand that change doesn't
come simply from thinking differently. The process involves
shifting what we understand, what we can feel, and what we
practice, reconnecting us with the incredible data and resilience of the body.

Somatics talks about the body as three billion years of
evolutionary wisdom. It's really more than the body in the
"Cartesian" view—body as object or machine. Somatics
brings an understanding and way to work with us as whole—
mind, beliefs, emotions, relations, resilience, adaptations, biology, meaning, and actions... All within and through the
body. And, that we are collective bodies as well. We transform
both individually and collectively.

The lineage of somatics that I am in, generative somatics,
puts an emphasis on somatics in the context of our social
conditions, and our efforts to create collective justice. We are
never just individual bodies, individual traumas—our lives
and the ways we survive are interconnected.

I first came across the work in 2009–2010, through a
collaboration called "Somatics and Social Justice." There was
clearly something really valuable in it, but also a lot of challenges about the course, and the trainers were transparent in
sharing that it was an experiment, that they were figuring

out how to best bridge the distance between somatics and social justice. That sense of transparent experimentation was exciting to me.

In 2012, I was invited into another course, "Somatics and Trauma." The course itself was solid, and I was really blown away by the palpable transformation in several of the teachers. I have seen and experienced a ton of leadership development processes, and most of them ultimately seem oriented around reproducing one person's way of being, which inevitably fails. This course was one of the first that I'd experienced that seemed to truly unlock people's power relative to their own potential.

I can't really tell you much about somatics, because it isn't about what we can say to each other, it's about what we can feel—of ourselves, of this world we belong to. It's about the correlation between feeling more and thus having more choices. I can say that, when it comes to adaptation, resilience through decentralization, interdependence, and other key elements of emergent strategy, somatics provides the best framework and practices that I have come across. Some of the aspects of it I most deeply align with include:

- Somatics is about being a fight *for*, rather than a fight *against*. Being in a fight for myself has led me to be honest about what makes me feel happy, strong, like I am realizing my miraculous potential. I've also looked at my friendships and relationships, asking myself how can I be a fight for my loved ones? This means not just listening to them, but listening for the truth within them, listening for what they are longing for, for what they know they deserve, for what they need. And showing up with them in that fight for their dignity, life, health, joy, self-realization. I am, again, so glad to be alive and awake at this moment as Black people fight for our dignity to be recognized, our lives to matter. There is so much to fight against, so many people who want us to cower and shrink, or, when we fight, to fight defensively, in isolation, against each other, to confirm some degrading concept of self, of Blackness, that has nothing to do with Black people, with evolving in our human purpose.

- Organizing and fortifying ourselves so that we can source from our longings, health, love, dreams, and visions, from our strength and our connections with each other.

- It is not about healing for the sake of individual wellness, though that is a radical act for any people slated for extinction. It is about healing trauma such that individuals and communities are not operating in reaction to oppression, and not relinquishing control over and over again because of changes outside their power.

- Increasing our agency is necessary—there is always going to be so much devastation to react to, especially for those of us on the wrong side of racism and oppression. The trauma won't stop. If we hope to advance, we have to find ways to move through and out of the vice grip of trauma that so drastically limits our choices.

- We say, "We don't practice to feel good, we practice to feel more."

As a student, I have done immense work on defining my purpose (including bringing these observations of emergent strategy forward), returning to my inherent dignity, and learning to stay present, open, and connected throughout my life.

As a teacher, I have watched room after room of movement organizers and workers drop into more authentic relationships with themselves and each other, increasing the transformation they can collectively leverage in their communities.

The aspects of somatics include somatic awareness, opening, and practices. It is an integrated way to change and become who we long to be, and be on an ongoing path. Generative somatics uses this work within movement organizations and alliances, and the practices and processes of embodied change get to happen there in the collective. The practices include aikido and other martial arts, meditation, physical training and coordination, and building new skills that are embodied (this means new options for responses and actions). Getting somatic bodywork done regularly lets what's stored in the body—emotions, habits, and survival strategies—process through…changing so much. This is done in a course or means working individually with a practitioner. It works to increase your ability to transform your own trauma through your body, and engage your history, resilience, and purpose.

Definitely seek out a generative somatics (gs) course near you—as part of the training community for gs, I can say we are working to increase the ways people can access this methodology directly from us.

Getting a bodyworker is the other best way into somatics.

Lisa Thomas-Adeyemo is our generative somatics song-bird and she once closed a session with this song, which keeps rolling through me:

> We gonna rise with the fire of freedom
> Truth is the fire that will burn our chains
> Stop the fire of destruction
> Healing is the fire running through our veins

"Fear and craving and hatred and clinging are deep emotional protections against the unknown that enabled us to survive over millions of years of evolution, and while we need to see how they hold us back, and learn how to overcome them—individually and collectively—we shouldn't pathologize them. We actually need to respect them."
—Jesse Maceo Vega Frey

Intimate Community on Social Media

I have found social media to be a sneaky place—it can be so comforting, and so distracting. It is the news and it is a bunch of unfounded random opinions and rants and TMI. I have wanted less randomness in my social-media use, and more depth; I want social media to flow with my life, rather than against, away from or over it. So over the past few years I have done a few experiments. There is a group that is now over a thousand people who are interested in Octavia Butler and Emergent Strategy explorations.[9] I love the things shared in that space. I have two other experiments that have become homes on the Internet. Below is a bit more about them, in the words of the participants.

1. Sugar Shift, on Facebook

THE INVITATION:

June 25, 2014: Welcome! My name is adrienne and I am a sugar addict with over thirty years in the game. This group is a supportive environment for myself and others who either self identify as sugar addicts, or in some other way recognize we need to be in active work to shift our relationships with sugar. That may include cleanses or longer term commitments to behavior change. This space is intended to increase accountability, process the real challenges, big up our successes, share recipes, and just keep learning. This process will follow emergent strategy because that is how I believe organic change happens. No failures, just data. Keep learning and self-loving!

PARTICIPANT TESTIMONIALS
(THE GROUP IS SECRET, BUT THESE LOVELY SHIFTERS GAVE ME TESTIMONIALS AND PERMISSION TO SHARE THEM!):

---

9   Thanks squad! This is me blowing a kiss to all of you who have cultivated the fire of geeking about all of this stuff with me, and especially for that one day you got me through.

Kenyetta Chinwe: This is the first space (online or in real life) that I've felt safe enough to be honest about my food struggles. Other groups I've been in either bombarded me with false encouragement or enabled me to continue in the behavior I was trying to adjust. This space has allowed me to be honest on the days I struggle, without allowing me to remain complacent. I am sure it is because of you all and your honesty that I'm now at my healthiest both physically and mentally that I've been in probably ten years. I love that, in this space, it is about being healthy and loving ourselves, not necessarily a particular way of eating other than sugar reduction. There seems to be little judgment either. We're able to explore what feels good to our bodies and share that without discrediting another's experience. That's the most valuable thing in this space to me.

Bilen Birhanu: The level of vulnerability and honesty in this space encouraged me to strip down and face the core of my life-long and pervasive struggle with food, especially sugar. The driving force of this community is the notion of shifting—there is no static or set destination, but a continual process of exploration, testing waters and learning new ways. Always learning. And leaning into the discomfort that comes with it.

Jane Brown: I feel more balance and I like that. And I want to go even deeper into this question we all have of "How do I face the ups & downs of life without diving head first into foods or patterns that are not healthy?" So, onward into Year 2 of Sugar Shift! And it really does feel like a "life shift" ... I don't at all feel like I'm "dieting" ... It's been a lifestyle change that I'm embracing! It's okay to ask for what you need! It's okay to say NO and it's okay to say YES when you're being intentional about what you eat/do! It's okay to do this the way it makes sense for YOU!

Supriya Lopez Pillai: adrienne and I haven't even seen each other in years. And, in this space of virtuality, I have grown closer to her and a bunch of other women, primarily, I don't even know. What the heck am I talking about? Sugar shifting. Back in September I declared myself a dedicated guinea pig to the experiment of ridding my diet of sugar. adrienne read my declaration on Facebook and invited me to a private group called Sugar Shift. It preceded me, it may have had a common history amongst its original shifters (perhaps a shared detox) but what I stepped into was a fantastic space of support with many who share similar politics, with some folks on the wagon, others off the wagon, some barely holding on by a thread, some totally ambivalent, but all at least thinking about the role sugar plays in our lives and how we all work toward freedom from its hold. Addiction as a metaphor (and a reality) is often raised. The various methods everyone is trying are shared in bits and pieces. Our victories and sidesteps are shared. What I love about the Sugar Shift group is we say, I've fallen down. Sometimes we are ok with being off of it. Sometimes we fell off and in coming back on we declare how much better we feel being back on. Whatever it is, it's a reminder that we are in it together. We stumble, we trip, we fall down, we get up. We stumble, we trip, we fall down, we get up. The body transforms, the mind transforms, everything transforms. Some people start with the mind, some people start with the body, some people start with communities. Whatever the case is, where you start and witness transformation—take it into all aspects of your life. Let it seep in.

2. Am I the Artist or Am I the Art? on Instagram

THE INVITATION:

March 2016: I am inviting a small crew of women and gender nonconforming friends into an experiment with each other, to share daily portraits of ourselves in this private thread for a month as a liberation technology, and affirm each other's beauty. Interested?

What happened:

There were six of us. I knew each person and wanted to know them better—they mostly didn't know each other. We shared daily self-portraits with each other in the spirit of Frida Kahlo (I was somewhat inspired by a picture of her, painting, that is floating around the Internet with the words "Never Be Ashamed of Your Selfies"). And we kind of all fell in love with each other. Halfway through, I realized that the month exactly overlapped with my month of being pregnant the year before. I was unaware of being pregnant until I was in the hospital losing it, so it was a gift that I spent the anniversary of that month in a daily practice of body celebration and awareness. These women were so generous—we shared pictures of joy and sadness, times we felt sexy and times we felt spent. What emerged was a community, a safe space, that is still very active today. Jay-Marie Hill, one of the participants, gathered some the things we said in affirmation of each other:

Jay-Marie: Appreciating the intricacies of y'alls realness, glows, and especially moments of slight defeat.

Sham-E-Ali Nayeem: It's a gift to share this space together in this moment in time. How fortunate am I to cross paths with each of you… I love you. Thank you for your gifts, creativity, and beauty.

dream hampton: I've really enjoyed being in community with y'all. Love to this whole beautiful crew.

Aja Taylor: I long ago stopped thinking of it as an experiment and more as a place I return to when I'm hungry for not food. It's just really wonderful being loved deeply in nonsexual ways. Perhaps the most beautiful shit ever. Especially when it's outside of people who are related to me by blood. It's my favorite part of life.

Nicole Newman: Do you know how powerful, how beautiful, how creative you are? Before the world beats no into your brow. Before heartbreak can be spotted in your eyes. Before your lips learn protection as a first language. Your creation was majestic. Your being enough. Do you know how enough you all are?

TOOLS FOR EMERGENT STRATEGY FACILITATION

"If you do not trust the people, they will become untrustworthy."
—Lao Tzu, *Tao Te Ching*

"I was very much interested in the way people behaved, the human dance, how they seemed to move around each other. I wanted to play around with that."
—Octavia Butler

In my mind, this is a book about facilitation. So I am ending with a last big evangelical burst of love for facilitation as a practice and toolset, a way of being with each other and in community in the world.

We are about to enter the smorgasbord-of-favorite-tools-for-facilitating section. These can be used within organizations, collectives, alliances, networks, and other formations. All of the following tools are either explicitly tools for emergent strategy, or can be adapted to work with the elements of emergent strategy.

There are four universal tools—Trust the People, Principles, Protocols, and Consensus—that just feel foundational. After that, I have grouped most of these tools by emergent strategy element, but feel free to liberate them and use them in any way that works for you!

Trust the People

One of the primary principles of emergent strategy is trusting the people. The flip of Lao Tzu's wisdom is: if you trust the people, they become trustworthy. Trust is a seed that grows with attention and space. The facilitator can be a gardener, or the sun, the water.

Often, facilitators seem to do the opposite of this. We sit with the organizers of a gathering and try to figure out ahead of time every single necessary conversation we want to see happen, and then create an agenda that imposes our priorities, or the organizers' priorities, on the people who we have invited to gather, ostensibly because we care about what they think, or about what they are doing.

Then, a few hours or days into the gathering, we are harried and desperate because the people have realized what we are up to, or simply aren't feeling heard, and/or we have missed something crucial that is at the center of the gathering. There emerges a sense of facilitators and participants working against each other, instead of everyone working in collaboration to meet the goals.

I have been experimenting with what it means to "trust the people" in practice.

I've been facilitating for a while, and although I know that the common wisdom is that every meeting has a flow of "form, storm, norm"—the group comes together, then explodes in opposition to what is happening and creates what they need, and then a norm emerges where there is a sense of accomplishment and deepening into their united identity—I have often wondered if there was another option, one that would save us time, resources, stress, division, and energy.

It's happening. Few of the meetings I have facilitated this past year have had a significant storm component. There has been tension, but it has been tension about the issues at hand, or larger interpersonal dynamics, the real struggles of movement. It hasn't been tension of people trying to find space to be heard and feel their time is well used.

To facilitate means to make it easy, and I feel like finally it is happening; it is getting easier for the participants and for me and my co-facilitators.

Here are some of the practices for trusting the people in practice.

1. Goal setting/intention.

Why are we meeting? What can this group uniquely accomplish? There are always a ton of relevant conversations that could happen, but there is usually a very small set of conversations that a particular group, at a particular moment in history, can have and move forward, given their capacity, resources, time, focus, and beliefs.

The organizers should have this question at the center of their planning for the event. I also find that it helps to survey the group of invitees to sharpen the goals, the desires people have for their time. The goals should be transparent, on the wall, in the room, referred to before closing the meeting. The goals are the north star and the way to assess satisfaction.

The goal can be relationship building—this is often the most necessary piece of work in terms of strengthening a group's resilience and capacity to move together. "Don't thingify," Taj offered me recently, when I was in a moment of pressure to produce "outcomes" at a large gathering. "Humanify! Shifting our way of being *is* our tangible outcome. Systems change comes from big groups making big shifts in being."

And remember, passion is a more valuable force for action and accountability than obligation, so let the goals be inspiring, uplifting what will inspire the most passionate conversation and participation.

2. Invite the right people.

We invite people to meetings for a lot of the wrong reasons—obligation, guilt, representation…even love. The questions to ask when shaping the invitation list are: "Who is directly impacted by this issue?"; "Who is doing compelling work on this issue?"; and "Who can move this work forward?"

Inviting the right people means we aren't wasting time by renegotiating the goals nonstop throughout the meeting and/ or managing the dissonance that occurs (righteously in my opinion) when a participant, who shouldn't be at the meeting, tries to make it worth their time by derailing the process of advancing the stated goals. Everyone should be able to be themselves and move their own agendas in the space if the invitation list is right.

Now, right people doesn't mean *easy* people—conflict and difference are often an important part of advancing the work, bringing the real issues into the room. Trust is built when the right people are in the right room, and can bring their opinions and work into a container that advances their individual and collective goals.

Inviting the right people also yields stronger relationships—people know why they are in the room with each other and are excited to do deeper work together. The connection between the individuals is what makes the whole group/community/effort strong.

The right facilitation team is also key. I love co-facilitating with people more creative and meticulous than me.

3. Individual participant articulation.

There are real language barriers—both literal and cultural—that mean we often think we are hearing each other, but we actually have no clue what others are saying. We all have filters, only some of which we are aware.

In a gathering, this can create the utmost confusion. Folks are using different cultural references, different touch points and acronyms, coming from widely different experiences and passions—even if what they are saying is similar, they can't hear and understand each other.

Giving everyone room to say what they want to prioritize and discuss, and then synthesizing that set of topics as a group, grows the common tongue of the participants, and allows for genuine clarity to happen in the dance of organizing all of the desires into a manageable number of conversations. My friend Allen Gunn taught me a way to do this with post-it notes and a blank wall, and I just keep iterating off of that exercise to create self-generated agendas.

When trying to determine which articulation to prioritize, go with that of the most impacted people in the room—it is usually the most relevant, and often the clearest and most accessible.

4. A living agenda.

Develop a spacious, adaptable agenda so the participants can shape the meeting.

Again, our tendency is to make use of the precious in-person time of a meeting by filling up every minute, from the beginning to the end of the day, with formal session time, creating schedules that are hard to change when new information comes along. These agendas are often burdened by an unrealistic hope, an underestimation of how long conversations may actually take.

Most conversations need at least 1.5 hours to adequately cover a basic orientation around the content, identify what is needed, and identify clear next steps. And that's conservative. Add an introduction round and you have a two- to three-hour conversation.

A meaningful full group conversation needs roughly five minutes per person. Underscheduling the amount of time a conversation needs means that energy will start to build up as people look for a way to release their thoughts and ideas into the group. Pair this with the power dynamics that often emerge—that some people feel really comfortable talking, and others don't—and you have a frustrating waste of time on your hands.

Folks are so used to not being heard. So used to not getting their needs met. When people feel heard, the time starts to expand as people move past expressing and start to be able to listen.

It is a beautiful thing to give people space and time, and, within the agenda, also point continuously towards collaboration. In the United States, where I do most of my facilitation, there is a socialized tendency towards competition—"My idea is the best and I am just here to sell it!" Well...no, thank you.

What can we do together from our passions?

Collaboration can only be built on relationships and shared vision. Relationships have to be respectful ("Oh, I totally see why you are here and why I would want to work with you") and real ("What you just said offended/disrespected me, and I can tell you about it because I want us to grow!"). And shared vision doesn't mean a ten-point shared utopia—it means you can generally state that you are moving in the same direction.

In agenda development, look for places where you can open people up to each other, and get their whole selves in the room. In my somatic studies, I am learning an immense amount about this opening, getting present, and connecting. It changes what is possible when people take the time to acknowledge they are whole selves in the room. It changes what is possible in a room when there is space for deepening one-on-one relationships as a way to build the strength of the whole room, early and often. Even a one-minute pairing exercise can increase the possibility of the room.

One more thing: the spacious agenda often leads to ending the meeting early, or right on time. There is always enough time for the right work. Try it! It's magical.

5. Listen with love!

The participants absolutely mean to be listening to each other, but their own agendas might fill up their ears with misunderstandings or frustrations. Your work as a facilitator is to listen to the needs of the group, help the participants to be clear to and with each other, and make sure you actually understand what folks in the room need.

Listen to the feedback you request that comes directly, and to the other feedback that flows in from the edges, the participants who need something more. My confession here is that I have, at times, grown annoyed with those participants who tend more towards deconstruction, anxiety, or frustration... They are the ones often less able to state clearly what they want. However, if I can drop in and set my annoyance aside, those folks are sometimes trying to get at the heart of the matter, or name the root schism in the room—the thing that is unnamed because it hard to name. Taking time to hear the participants in the margins of the agenda can actually help get the event on point. And I can't count the number of times a disgruntled participant was actually just misunderstanding something that, when clarified, made them a star participant.

There is a conversation in the room that wants and needs to be had. Don't force it, don't deny it. Let it come forth.

6. Know when to say yes and when to say no.

Yes to those things that deepen the gathering—cultural grounding, local welcome, clarifying questions, learning in real time, suggestions to slow down. No to manipulative efforts to quiet others, pontification, ignorance.

Yes to singing, bio breaks (bathroom, fresh air, snacks, self care), ending early (when the group has run out of energy for the day), talent shows, parties, and efforts to synthesize.

No to judgment, delays, circular conversations, and people who are rejecting the process while offering no alternatives.

And yes to passion, no to obligation. Good ideas become great movement growth strategies with the touch of passionate hands and work. Ideas that emerge from obligation tend to go stagnate waiting for water.

7. Don't hover!

Give the group time to be in its own process, conversation, or small group without your intervention. Be available if needed, but make room. This allows the group to actually problem solve together, develop relationships, and cultivate each other's leadership.

8. What you gonna do?

Gibrán Rivera once articulated a question to me: "What is the next most elegant step?"

I love this question and use it to shape conversations all the time. Too often we come up with plans that don't take into account the fog on the horizon. Then we go off and the work doesn't happen, perhaps can't happen, and then we feel demoralized when our energy doesn't flow into action or desired outcomes.

An elegant step is one that acknowledges what is known and unknown, and what the capacity of this group actually is. An elegant step allows humility, allows people to say "Actually we need to do some research" or "Actually we need to talk to some folks not in this room" or "Actually we need a full day to build this plan out into something realistic and attainable."

In any conversation—and I would say in any moment in life—there is a next elegant step—one that is possible and strategic based on who is taking it and where they are trying to go. Find it and you cannot fail.

Develop a strategic direction moving towards vision, determining appropriate tactics based on the horizon you can see. Move forward with awareness. Develop strategic bodies and minds to adapt intelligently as the horizon changes.

"As humans we are part of nature. Our basic physical needs/instincts as mammals and our natural basic emotional needs are often in conflict with our abilities to think complex thoughts and build complex things. One way in which an understanding of human nature influences my organizing is that I've learned that, as humans, we are operating at the level of basic instinct more than we know. We are always ensuring that our basic needs are met and that our emotional selves are nurtured. We're often trying to escape our nature as we try to commune with technology, and these forces are in tension. In my organizing, I've learned to look for the simple, basic human that is at the core of every big vision and complex idea or system. Whenever someone I'm working with advocates for something complex, I pause and see them as the fragile human that they are, really fulfilling their nature vis à vis self preservation and healing. I understand that the project or idea is important to this person not just at the complex organizational level but at the deeply personal, instinctual level as well. This helps me connect with them and have increased empathy."
—Aisha Shillingford

PRINCIPLES

My favorite way that adaptation with intention and interdependence get practiced is through shared principles. Having clear principles or intentions means, that as conditions change, there is a common understanding of what matters, a way to return to shared practice and behavior.

Allied Media Projects (AMP) has principles that have deeply moved me since I first heard of them—they represent adaptation in how they were created as well as in their content. Here's what AMP says about their principles, followed by the principles themselves:

> Since its inception in 2002 and going back to the initial conference in 1999, Allied Media Projects has been learning from its network of participants. Through the (annual) Allied Media Conference vision statement, case statement, and conference program, we attempt to articulate what we learn back to the network each year, continuing the process of listening and learning and speaking. We adapt our way of organizing based on what we hear and learn from the network.
>
> Year to year, many things have changed and continue to change, giving our shared work and the conference vitality. Especially in the past few years, though, we have drawn certain lessons repeatedly, from a variety of sources. Together, we have tested, adapted, applied, and honed these lessons. At this point, some of the concepts are so consistent and widely practiced throughout the network, that they amount to a set of shared principles. We articulate these shared principles here, to the best of our ability, so that we can all more clearly understand the work we are doing together...

> - We are making an honest attempt to solve the most significant problems of our day.
> - We are building a network of people and organizations that are developing long-term solutions based on the immediate confrontation of our most pressing problems.
> - Wherever there is a problem, there are already people acting on the problem in

some fashion. Understanding those actions is the starting point for developing effective strategies to resolve the problem, so we focus on the solutions, not the problems.

- We emphasize our own power and legitimacy.
- We presume our power, not our powerlessness.
- We are agents, not victims.
- We spend more time building than attacking.
- We focus on strategies rather than issues.
- The strongest solutions happen through the process, not in a moment at the end of the process.
- The most effective strategics for us arc the ones that work in situations of scarce resources and intersecting systems of oppression because those solutions tend to be the most holistic and sustainable.
- Place is important. For the AMC, Detroit is important as a source of innovative, collaborative, low-resource solutions. Detroit gives the conference a sense of place, just as each of the conference participants bring their own sense of place with them to the conference.
- We encourage people to engage with their whole selves, not just with one part of their identity.
- We begin by listening.

"The one thing I've learned from nature that influences how I organize the most is that I have to listen. The Allied Media Projects principles begin with listening, but I think it goes farther than that for me. I have to listen to others who have worked on similar struggles to me for far longer than I have. I have to set aside my ego and my will and even my desire and listen to what the goddess wants, and when I do that I am living in my greatest purpose, which sometimes looks like radical self care and currently looks like a devotion to my own health and healing, but at other times looks like sharing my story, or like dreaming up new galaxies, or like working with others to birth new realities together."

—micha cárdenas

Jemez Principles for Democratic Organizing

There are many other sets of principles that are core to a lot of the work I do—here are the Jemez Principles for Democratic Organizing,[1] which many groups I work with hold core to our work:

On December 6–8, 1996, forty people of color and European-American representatives met in Jemez, New Mexico, for the "Working Group Meeting on Globalization and Trade." The Jemez meeting was hosted by the Southwest Network for Environmental and Economic Justice, with the intention of hammering out common understandings between participants from different cultures, politics, and organizations. The following "Jemez Principles" for democratic organizing were adopted by the participants:

#1 Be Inclusive:

If we hope to achieve just societies that include all people in decision making and assure that all people have an equitable share of the wealth and the work of this world,

---

1   http://www.ejnet.org/ej/jemez.pdf

then we must work to build that kind of inclusiveness into our own movement in order to develop alternative policies and institutions to the treaties policies under neo-liberalism. This requires more than tokenism, it cannot be achieved without diversity at the planning table, in staffing, and in coordination. It may delay achievement of other important goals, it will require discussion, hard work, patience, and advance planning. It may involve conflict, but through this conflict, we can learn better ways of working together. It's about building alternative institutions, movement building, and not compromising out in order to be accepted into the anti-globalization club.

#2 Emphasis on Bottom-Up Organizing:

To succeed, it is important to reach out into new constituencies, and to reach within all levels of leadership and membership base of the organizations that are already involved in our networks. We must be continually building and strengthening a base which provides our credibility, our strategies, mobilizations, leadership development, and the energy for the work we must do daily.

#3 Let People Speak for Themselves:

We must be sure that relevant voices of people directly affected are heard. Ways must be provided for spokespersons to represent and be responsible to the affected constituencies. It is important for organizations to clarify their roles, and who they represent, and to assure accountability within our structures.

#4 Work Together In Solidarity and Mutuality:

Groups working on similar issues with compatible visions should consciously act in solidarity, mutuality and support each other's work. In the long run, a more significant step is to incorporate the goals and values of other groups with your own work, in order to build strong relationships. For instance, in the long run, it is more important that labor unions and community economic development projects include the issue of environmental sustainability in their own strategies, rather than just lending support to the environmental organizations. So communications, strategies and resource sharing is critical, to help us see our connections and build on these.

#5 Build Just Relationships Among Ourselves:

We need to treat each other with justice and respect, both on an individual and an organizational level, in this country and across borders. Defining and developing "just relationships" will be a process that won't happen overnight. It must include clarity about decision-making, sharing strategies, and resource distribution. There are clearly many skills necessary to succeed, and we need to determine the ways for those with different skills to coordinate and be accountable to one another.

#6 Commitment to Self-Transformation:

As we change societies, we must change from operating on the mode of individualism to community-centeredness. We must "walk our talk." We must be the values that we say we're struggling for and we must be justice, be peace, be community.

Protocols Across Community and Formation

Protocols are ways that principles look in action—the actual order, boundaries, practices, and paths towards being in principle.

The first time I heard about protocols was while working with Indigenous communities through the Indigenous People's Power Project. I was so moved by the clarity of the protocols—in each community there are ways to honor and respect the culture, the elders, the leadership, the history, and the power dynamics.

I have also been pleased to experience protocols being practiced in intersectional ally work. Protocol for working together,[2] protocol for taking action together. There was a set of protocols articulated by the team at Ruckus, protocols intended to shift the practices of parachuting in and out of communities, using communities as the backdrop of outsiders' issues and campaigns. We wanted to center community in direct actions that grew their power. It's thrilling to see how many hands and minds have shaped these protocols to suit this bursting forth movement moment.

Bay Area Solidarity Action Team (BASAT) and #Asians4BlackLives (A4BL) are two ally groups that both have really powerful principles and protocols that guide their choices and actions. I am including excerpts from both, and encourage you to visit their sites, read (and use) the full text!

First an excerpt from BASAT:[3]

> This is a living document that will continue to evolve. The foundation for this protocol came from The Ruckus Society's Action Framework.
>
> **Protocol & Principles for White People Working to Support the Black Liberation Movement:**
>
> Frontline Leadership
>
> Solidarity is a Verb
>
> Long Haul Relationships
>
> Centering Blackness
>
> Don't Let Whiteness Get in the Way
>
> Stay Human, Stay Grounded: Our own liberation is bound to the liberation of Black people. We will stay emotionally connected to the gravity of the war on Black people.
>
> Visionary and Confrontational Action: We commit to taking action that holds space for community vision, aligns with national

---

2   www.ejnet.org/ej/workingtogether.pdf.

3   To find the full protocol and principles for BASAT, visit baysolidarity .wordpress.com.

demands from FergusonAction, and places our bodies in the path of injustice.

Tactical Discipline

Reflection ←—→ Action cycle: We will constantly evaluate and learn from our mistakes and strengths, and share learning with others.

Sustainability

And here are some excerpts from #Asians4BlackLives's principles and protocols:[4]

> We are a diverse group of Asian voices coming from the Philippines, Vietnam, India, China, Pakistan, Korea, Burma, Japan, and other nations, based in the Bay Area. We are mothers and fathers, sisters and brothers, educators and organizers, students and teachers, artists and techies, dancers and workers, youth and elders. We are immigrant and U.S. born, we are queer and we are straight, we are many genders, we are families. From our many walks of life, we have come together in response to a call from Black Lives Matter Bay Area (including the BlackOut Collective, Black Brunch organizers, Onyx Organizing Committee, and more) and the larger Black Lives Matter movement, to put forward these principles and protocols as a model for why and how we, as diverse Asian communities around the country and the world, can show up in solidarity with Black people in this struggle.

---

4   To find the full protocol and principles for A4BL, visit: a4bl.wordpress .com.

PROTOCOLS:

How we believe in doing this work

Organize Our People

Strive for a strategic diversity of tactics so all who want *can* play a role

Build Trust & Practice Transparency

Move Boldly and Swiftly: Take Risks, Make Mistakes, Share Lessons

Embody self care & humility, community accountability, collective healing

We submit these principles and protocols with humility and openness. We don't have it all figured out, but we are committed to taking a stand, and learning as we go. We will not wait to be perfect, because we believe the time is now and we would rather be held accountable for our mistakes than forgiven our inaction.

Group Agreements

At the beginning of a meeting of people who don't work together regularly, it helps to set some agreements in place. If people are working together regularly, just have some standing agreements. Here are some of my favorites for emergent spaces:

- Listen from the inside out, or listen from the bottom up (a feeling in your gut matters!);
- Engage Tension, Don't Indulge Drama;
- W.A.I.T.—Why Am I Talking?
- Make Space, Take Space—a post-ableist adaptation of step up, step back to help balance the verbose and the reticent;[5]

---

5   Learned from Cinna, at Extreme Energy Extraction Summit, a twice yearly gathering of communities resisting extreme energy extraction around the globe.

- Confidentiality—take the lessons, leave the details;
- Be open to learning;
- Be open to someone else speaking your truth;
- Building, not selling—when you speak, converse, don't pitch;
- Yes/and, both/and;
- Value the process as much as, if not more than, you value the outcomes;
- Assume best intent, attend to impact;
- Self care and community care—pay attention to your bladder, pay attention to your neighbors.

Efficient Consensus Decision Making

I love to say the words "consensus decision making" to people who use the words "efficient" and "ASAP" to describe everything good. The response face is similar to when a baby tastes lemon for the first time.

I think people imagine being in the movie *12 Angry Men* when they hear the word "consensus"—no bathroom breaks, endless hero sandwiches, wearing each other down to the least interesting decision.

What I mean when I say it is: make sure the people who will be doing the work agree on what is being done, why and how. This is the heart of efficiency—that there is nothing dragging or diverting the energy of the work. When people agree to work, but don't really understand it or support it, they slowly become a counterforce—doing the work slowly, or without their full positive attention, or explicitly sabotaging the work. A bit more clarity on the front end builds trust and alignment within the group.

These are core elements of consensus decision making that are crucial in resilient, decentralized organizations:[6]

---

6   I learned these tools from Autumn Meghan Brown, whose work can be found at www.iambrown.org. She is also interviewed on consensus and other things earlier in this book.

Proposal-based decisions.

Those who have worked with me as a facilitator know that I can get too excited about proposal-based decision making. I am not ashamed. It hurts me to hear a group spin in a circle, unsure if a decision has been made, or if they even know what they are deciding to do, or if they are making a decision at all, perhaps it's just a conversation. Does this feel at all familiar?

Example 1

"Hey I really don't like you using bottled water cause you know plastic build up in the ocean hurts dolphins, whales, and the future."

"I feel you. I just don't trust the government to provide clean water and buying bottles is easier than using charcoal."

"Can we just buy a water filter for the faucet though?"

"Probably Sue in HR could do that."

Next meeting:

"I'm really angry you're still using bottled water. I guess everyone here hates the Earth."

"Look, until there is a filter I am gonna drink clean water from this plastic bottle!"

"Hey guys, did one of you talk to Sue in HR about this?"

"No, I thought that guy over there was going to."

"But he has a charcoal filter bottle and wasn't even in that conversation."

Rage. Resignations.

It doesn't have to be that way. Here's another option:

Example 2

"Hey everyone, I'd like to change our water system from bottled water to something more in line with our values."

"Oh yeah? Let's have a brief discussion at this week's staff meeting to explore options and preferences to stop using bottled water, and you develop a proposal based on that. If you send it to us by Wednesday we'll review it and decide during next week's staff meeting."

"Sounds good."

"Great—make sure Sue will be at the meeting, this is her area of work."

"Roger that, homeboyyyyy!" (Or however y'all end conversations.)

The proposal-based method has three basic steps:

1. Identify the area where a decision is needed and have an exploratory conversation to find out where the group's preferences and concerns are.
   - Best practice: make room for brainstorm-level ideas from the group, saying yes to all the ideas. Some folks, more than will admit it, feel shut down if their ideas are being debated and shot down as they speak.
2. Based on that conversation and any additional research, one person or sub-group can develop a proposal that represents the discussion.
   - Best practices:
     ○ Structure a proposal that says what you want to do, why it serves the mission/vision of the group, and who/what/when/where/how it will happen.
     ○ Send out a written version of it for folks to review. (Giving people time to review the proposal ahead of time *really* helps reduce knee-jerk reactions and increase thoughtful, informed decision making.)
3. Review proposal together and make decision.[7] Once

---

7   When getting started with this method, or if working with a large group, I recommend using a system called fist-five for voting, where people use their hands or call out a number from zero to five to indicate their level of agreement with the proposal. Anything less than a five calls for some discussion, and you move a proposal forward if the participants are all above a three, or above a four, depending on the

the proposal is reviewed in real time (in person or over phone/video), first get responses to any clarifying questions, then have a discussion of whether this proposal serves the group at this moment. The exploratory conversation before generating the proposal generally increases the chances of a successful proposal, but stay open to friendly amendments.

- There are a couple of possibilities for how things go at this point:
  - Outcome A: Everyone feels great about the proposal, it reflects the conversation and cares of the group. There is an affirmation of the proposal.
  - Outcome B: People feel mostly good about the proposal but have some amendments. In brief conversation offer these amendments.
    - Best practices:
      - Put the basic elements of the proposal up where everyone can see them with room to note the amendments. For some folks, having a conversation without something they can see gets really confusing.
      - If you are making the amendment, be clear in your self and in your words as to whether the amendment is a suggestion or a requirement without which you will not approve the proposal.
  - Outcome C: People have major changes or a different direction they want to go in.
    - Best practices:
      - have that person/group take

nature of your group. See additional resources for this in the documents accompanying this book at alliedmedia.esii.

responsibility for developing a counter proposal.

- It also helps if there is a brief moment to examine what happened between the exploratory conversation and this moment. Does the proposal not represent the conversation? Did this person not speak up during the conversation? Learn from what happened to strengthen the proposal method moving forward. Be alert for these kind of participants...and try not to be this kind of participant:
  - "the people who have THE BEST AND ONLY IMPORTANT IDEAS and are not interested at all in being amenable, let alone compromising for the sake of finding a collective agreement"— thank you Clare Bayard for naming this so clearly;[8]
  - the person who was texting or otherwise occupied during all the crucial proposal considerations;
  - the wordsmith, who basically agrees with the proposal but wants to change all the words, or examine what IS is;
  - the lazy proposer. They bring a proposal but don't think it through, which means the work ends up back in the group's lap;
  - the Eeyore worrywart. This

---

8   This person should figure out work they can do solo that contributes to the movement :)

           person can only think in worst-case scenarios, their mind racing ahead of the conversation to that day in the future when it all inevitably goes to hell;

- the passive-aggressive person who won't come out and say they don't agree with proposal, but keep asking questions to delay decision making;
- the devil's advocate.[9]

   o Outcome D: Block! One or more people in the group block the process from moving forward. Blocks should be saved for moments when there is a real ideological struggle for the group, i.e. "This proposal would put us at odds with our core values." If a block happens in this process, it means there is a communication breakdown somewhere along the path and it's time to slow down and get to the bottom of it!

Being honest about your level of agreement.

We like to be nice, supportive, agreeable and stuff. In some places, politeness is the cultural norm. This sometimes leads to us saying yes to things that we actually don't agree with and have no intention of working on, or moving forward as a group on a proposal that we know is too flawed to work. That leads to inefficiency as things we don't want to do slip down our to-do lists, or as we run into problems that everyone could foresee, or in extreme cases, as we work against the very things we said yes to.

There are lovely and quick tools for measuring levels of agreement—thumbs up or down, or letting the number of

---

9   "Get thee behind me Satan!"

fingers you hold up correlate to level of agreement.[10] I highly recommend using these, at least initially. Like training wheels. Eventually in most groups, you develop your own rhythm and code for this. Some groups only move forward when everyone is all in. Others do modified versions of consensus. The key is cultivating transparency, honesty in the decision-making process.

A clear no.

When a group is scared of saying "no," it quickly ends up spread too thin. "No" is as important to realizing your vision as "yes." There is a lot of work that is not yours to do. There are millions and millions of people at work. "No" creates the space for your "yes." "No" also creates the space for other groups to do the things you can't, and to do them with enough time and focus and expertise to do them well.

After reading an early draft of this book, Clare Bayard added this, which feels important: "This section could set up a false expectation that if you write a good proposal, it should be hella smooth—and even that smooth is the goal, so if there is contention, that means you/the group failed. Consensus, at its best, is a process that helps a group to do its best thinking—in that way that all of us know something and together we know a lot—and sometimes arriving at decisions, solutions, or plans is complicated (and I want people to anticipate that with joy!)…"

Facilitation Tools for Adaptation

Developing Strategic Intentions

Think of strategic intentions as a north star. I see strategic plans as maps through territory—maps that can be out of date the moment they are written down as the political,

10 You can find additional resources and visuals for consensus decision making at http://i.imgur.com/FEEpW.png.

economic, or social landscapes shift like tectonic plates. It's great to have the map and apply past wisdom and experience to planning how to get from point A to point B, but there are larger systems that are less mutable, that are like stars, grand and steady in the landscape. Why not use those as a directional guide as well, a way to adapt in real time while still holding direction?

While she didn't use this exact language, Jidan Koon, a comrade facilitator, taught me a lot about strategic intentions while I worked at Ruckus.

First, she helped us as an organization see that we needed to prune, to get to our essential work. She literally drew a tree that was clearly overgrown and having a hard time holding itself up, each of the branches representing parts of our work. Then she drew a tree that was spare, balanced, solid, deeply rooted.

We had a long-view vision of communities experiencing power, liberation, and sustainability; and we had a clear mission, meaning we knew how we would achieve our vision— radical direct action by, with, and for directly impacted communities. Jidan helped us identify values aligned with our work, values that we needed to grow within the organization's practices and partnerships—our strategic intentions.

Our core strategic intention became sustainability—we assessed the entire organization based on how sustainable each aspect of our structure and work were, and came up with an organization-wide plan of action, a standard we could hold up in decision making. Over time, this led to focusing our programs, downsizing the staff, investing more in the network of trainers and organizers that are the backbone of the organization, and developing an action protocol about when and how we entered a community.

It didn't all happen at once, of course, but with time it emerged from the strategic intention to embody sustainability.

Since then I have facilitated many groups in this kind of strategic intention setting. Here are the basic steps I use:

Vision

The vision of an organization is the furthest it can see. It is looking into the future, dreaming together, predicting impact, flexing the imagination muscle, and saying aloud what we long for. I cannot overstate this—the more people who deeply share a vision, the more possible that vision becomes. Build the vision across your group.

When new people come in, make sure they are already deeply aligned with the vision (they could easily say "This is MY vision"), or take the time to orient and align. If you bring on a number of new people, it may mean revisiting the vision. I recommend an annual check in on the vision—is this still the furthest we can see?

Octavia's Brood has been leading Collective Sci-Fi Writing workshops around the country, and these are one way to get a group of people to articulate a shared vision: by picking an issue and writing visionary fiction for it as a medicine.[11]

You can easily search for visioning exercises. I love the time-travel newspaper headline exercise for finding the common ideas that bring everyone together.[12] I also love having people draw their visions with crayon and colored pencils, place them together on a wall or table, and then articulate the patterns they see in the drawings as a group.

What I will add is that I think it's really important to also clarify the places where there is *not* alignment on vision—be

---

11   You can book workshops at https://www.alliedmedia.org/octavias-brood/booking.

12   You imagine yourself in the future (set a date that people can imagine—twenty years out, say), walking to work, and you see a newspaper. You pick it up and the headline is celebrating the work of your organization/group/movement. Recreate the front page: What paper is it? Is it a hologram? What is the headline? Picture? Leading article? Put the front pages up on a wall where everyone can see each other's vision—discuss the patterns and longings that your future headlines unveil.

really clear about what is and what is not part of the shared collective vision of the group.

In a migration metaphor: if everyone else is set on migrating to Mexico, and you really want to end up in Chile, you may need to find a different flock eventually, and it's good to know that. I am a fan of multiverse theory, that there are parallel universes for everything we can imagine, or every choice we make. I reject the idea that there is ever only one way forward at an individual or collective level.

That said, an organization is a specific and strange thing, like a *Flintstones* vehicle—it moves based on the aligned energy of those powering it from within. So, know where you're heading.

Technically, this means that however you do the visioning work, once you brainstorm the elements of vision in a way that everyone can look at the ideas together, ask the group to do the brave work of crossing off those words that don't represent their vision. Only the words that remain will grow, because those are the places of actual alignment.

Some groups get caught up in attending to the places where they aren't aligned. What I have seen work best over the years is for groups to be aware of where they aren't aligned, but to focus on and grow the areas of alignment. The larger the alignment is, the more room there is for contradiction and difference. And, if need be, for moving in different directions with integrity.

A small point on this—we can only see so far, literally and in our collective imaginations. So it's also good to be aware that you may be setting your vision based on the horizon you can see, and as you move towards it, it will change.

The gift is, it keeps going.

On this planet there are as many horizons as there are places to be (stand, sit, fly, etc.) x 360 degrees x seconds of the day. I am not fluent in math, but that seems to be a pretty massive number of horizons! So hold the vision, and know that as you grow, as you move towards it, the vision will adapt too.

Example: One of my favorite visions of all time is from Generation Five, working to end childhood sexual abuse in five generations. They fleshed out their five-generation vision with outcomes for each generation, and it feels so thorough, so achievable.[13]

Mission

Once you identify the vision, you want to choose the vehicle. Is it the Flintstone's Cadillac or the Flintstone's Rav4? A bike? A mindmeld?

For example, your vision is a world with no prisons. You can approach that with policy-change advocacy work, with direct action inside and outside of prisons, with education, with mediation circles in the community, or many other options. In truth, all of those methods in combination are needed. But they are very, very different methods, and it might be hard to do all of those well in one vehicle. Identifying what your group can do well, is passionate about, and is needed— that's the sweet spot.

That's your mission.

Your mission should be brief and clear, so that you can refer to it at moments of decision, at forks in your organizational road. It should resonate with everyone in the organization, a compelling statement that makes everyone want to show up and kick ass.

Here are some good mission statements:

"Movement Generation Justice & Ecology Project inspires and engages in transformative action towards the liberation and restoration of land, labor, and culture. We are rooted in vibrant social movements led by low-income communities and communities of color committed to a Just Transition away from profit and pollution and towards healthy, resilient and life-affirming local economies."

---

13   You can read the full vision at alliedmedia.org/esii.

"The Ruckus Society provides environmental, human rights, and social justice organizers with the tools, training, and support needed to achieve their goals through the strategic use of creative, nonviolent direct action."

"Allied Media Projects cultivates media strategies for a more just, creative and collaborative world. We serve a network of media makers, artists, educators, and technologists working for social justice."

"Black Lives Matter is a chapter-based national organization working for the validity of Black life. We are working to (re)build the Black liberation movement."

"BOLD (Black Organizing for Leadership and Dignity) is a national Leadership Training Program designed to help rebuild Black (African-American, Caribbean, African, Afro-Latino) social justice infrastructure in order to organize Black communities more effectively and re-center Black leadership in the U.S. social justice movement."

Strategic Intentions!

"Water has taught me how to be in the flow, to release and cleanse what no longer serves me or us. There is power in letting go what is not ours to carry, or what others in their unskillfulness, have tried to place upon us."
—Brenda Salgado

What do you need to do or be great at to embody your vision as you fulfill your mission? Brainstorm a huge list of things, go nuts.

Cluster those things. You might have sustainability things, or stuff related to conflict resolution, community leadership, decision making, financial management or fundraising, visibility and communications, or totally other stuff. Clustering helps you get a first glance at what is showing up.

Now prioritize the clusters.

The biggest clusters may not be the most necessary, just the most obvious. You want to be intentional as a group, and I like "dotmocracy" for this—everyone gets two or three "votes" in the forms of a sticker (a dot, a star, a unicorn), or just a mark. Everyone goes up and marks their top priorities (with one sticker per choice, or putting all their marks on their top choice). Prioritization is important because even if you *know* all the things that would create perfect vision embodiment, unless you are a crew of gifted superhumans, you can't *do* all the things at once. If you try that, your default behaviors will easily resist your efforts to change.

Prioritize for what I call the "first domino" cluster, the thing that, if you achieve it, will begin to move the whole pattern.

Example: I mentioned that for Ruckus one of our strategic intentions was sustainability. This was because, in a state of organizational burnout, nothing else was achievable. I suspect many organizations are like this, needing to get a sustainable internal culture both because it aligns with long-term vision and because everything else is impossible from that state of perpetual flame.

Task it out. Yes this can be a work plan! For the work you can foresee, what needs to be done? Who will do it? By when?[14] Get it mapped out to your heart's content—just know it may change.

Guiding statements or questions!

Guiding statements or guiding questions can be really helpful for adapting while staying intentional. These are the

---

14   Throughout this book, I touch on shared work management systems that liberate the information about where tasks are in organizations. See especially the "Tools for Emergent Strategy Facilitation" chapter in the section "Tools for Increasing Interdependence and Decentralization."

words that remind you to look up, look ahead, your north star words.

For Ruckus, part of growing our sustainability was working with groups that really wanted our presence, rather than expending energy trying to push into spaces where we weren't invited. We learned as a national organization that it was more sustainable and more aligned with all of our values to trust local work, and to come when we were called, rather than parachuting in on the strength of our own interests. When potential action opportunities came up, we asked each other, "Who is calling for us?," making sure the directly impacted community actually wanted us there.

For the Detroit Narrative Agency, a project dedicated to shifting the common narratives about Detroit away from "blank slate/canvas" and "violent crime city" to "popular resistance against injustice" and "resilient long-lasting communities," with the understanding that the future of a place follows the stories we tell about that place.[15] As we have moved through the work we keep asking ourselves, "What is the narrative being uplifted here? And who is sharing that narrative?"

Facilitation Tools for Nonlinear/Iterative

Post-it Planning

This is so simple and so exactly what it sounds like. I am a big fan of having a visual and written depiction of shared work. What is the task, when will it be done, who is doing it? Being able to quickly look at a shared plan can reduce confusion and conflict once the work begins.

The key to embracing non-linear and iterative work is being able to easily shift the moving parts. And some wonderful person created post-it notes for this purpose.[16] When making

---

15   Learn more about the work of the Detroit Narrative Agency at https://www.alliedmedia.org/dna.

16   Arthur Fry co-invented the Post-it Note.

a plan with others, use a wall or a big piece of paper as a time-line, and use post-its for each task, event, milestone. This way the timeline can easily be adjusted when change happens.

While I was at Ruckus, my coworker Hannah Strange once set this up with handmade horse-shaped post-its that were each separate projects racing through tasks towards a finish line. Get creative.

Circular Agendas

I started using these as I became more comfortable with emergent strategy because I was tired of having tight time-bound agendas that pretended the work we were doing could be predicted ahead of time, and then inevitably changed because humans showed up for the meeting.

What I have found is that, if we are doing the right work, the timing works out. We structure the time, and we protect the time we have together by cultivating a culture of starting and ending on time, but inside the time, the time expands and shape shifts for the work that is needed. The clarity is around the goals, and the arc of the work.

The circular agenda shows that there is a continuous arc to the work we are doing, and presents the suggestion for when and how that arc will flow, but it also allows for things to move and for everyone to focus on the importance of the flow more than on the time slots.

Before developing the agenda at all, I work with as many people in the group as I can access in order to get a solid grasp on the goals/intentions for the meeting. Often the agenda gets disrupted because there are divergent in-tentions in the room, and not enough space provided for alignment work. So getting clear on the shared intentions (often called goals) and places (or hot spots, turbulence, bumps, landmines, or other explosive words depending on the setting) where we can expect discussion will be needed for alignment.

I advocate for an agenda that is spacious. This often means negotiating with the group/organizers about what can and cannot be accomplished in the time they have set aside for the meeting. Giving an agenda adequate space and room for human interaction and discussion often leads to significantly more ground getting covered in an authentic way in the time available.

I often work with the co-facilitators and organizers of the meeting/gathering to create a detailed step-by-step planned out agenda and hold onto this as a facilitation agenda, which I can refer to throughout the process and make sure we are covering all the bases.

In the room, I structure the agenda on butcher paper like a clock, beginning at the top (midnight/noon) and circling around clockwise. (It doesn't *need* to be a circle, but that does seem to help people see the space of the meeting as a finite time within a larger arc of change. And it's such a sacred shape in our universe—it's an orbit, a moon cycle, time.) I use large chunks of time—morning, afternoon—and place in those chunks the work that will most likely happen during that time. I often check off pieces of work as we go, so there is a transparent understanding in the room of what we are moving through.

The idea is to make room for the conversations that need to be had—to look ahead as clearly as possible, to tune into the feelings of unity or tension in the room, and to consistently be lining up the work with the intentions of the group and of this particular meeting. Taj often says that for each group, each convergence of people, there is a conversation or a set of work that only *that* group can have or do, and the work of the facilitator and group is honing in on that specific work and doing it, having those conversations.

Individual and Collective Reflection

Taking the time to reflect on the changes that are taking place is crucial for understanding nonlinear and iterative growth. It may seem like nothing is changing, and then you look back and see that you have become a different person, or group, entirely.

Cindy Wiesner[17] once spoke of this as digestion time. We were working with a group that was trying to reach consensus about a complex proposal, and she suggested scheduling in periods of reflection after each segment of the proposal in order for folks to digest what they were working on.

A lot of conflict and discontent in organizations comes because we don't build in time and space for this digestion—to really understand each other across difference, to understand ideas and opinions that are not our own, to move past the initial knee-jerk reaction, shaped by our unique socialization and experience, and into reflection.

This is cellular, the individual or collective body is constantly renewing, new understanding is attained through repetition of practices, change is constant.

I recommend that any group of people working together over time schedule regular time for reflecting on and evaluating the work done, harvesting the lessons and applying them to future iterations of the work.

For organizations, I recommend three or four annual advances. (Calling them "retreats" when they are work sessions is disingenuous. Plan retreats too! Just don't confuse them.) One can focus on reflection and evaluation; one can focus on applying lessons from reflection to the next period of time (planning); and one can be about big vision, meta discussions of the work, the field, the patterns emerging, skill development. Looking back, looking ahead, looking up and down.

You can also mix these together so each advance has these elements. Just stay in touch with the whole vision inside the work.

17　Cindy is one of the most dynamic organizers of our time. Her work is primarily around climate—she works at Grassroots Global Justice, is part of the Climate Justice Alliance—and I had the opportunity to work with her on the second US Social Forum in 2010.

Flow and Toolbox

When I am facilitating small groups (less than ten people, who are fairly familiar with each other), I often use a method I think of as flow and toolbox:

- List the topics that need discussion.
- For each section I have participants write/reflect/draw their thoughts on blank paper.
- Have participants briefly share their reflections, then discuss it all as a group, pulling out patterns, themes, principles together.
- As it makes sense, I draw things out of my toolbox to offer up and support the group. For instance, we might pause to review consensus, or I might show them how Basecamp or OpenOffice works (online work management tools).
- At the end of the discussion of each topic, we generate take-aways and identify someone to turn our conversation into a clear proposal for next steps.
- At the end of the day, review and balance next steps, making sure the load is shared amongst the group.

"One time I went walking among the Redwoods in this park. There was all of this information about how the trees take care of themselves. You could see how every species living in the area was related to and reliant on each other. The whole place was full of triumphs, sacrifices. Full of beauty accumulated over centuries, and the remains of unexpected disasters. A true collaboration of all the elements that all living things need to sustain life on this planet. So many living things thriving and so many dead things being absorbed back into the earth. That is a powerful system, older than anything I know. It has to be saved from poachers or it wouldn't exist in these times. I learned to try

to organize in collaboration with what is around
me and to try to leave something useful for those
yet to come. I have to live, organize, work with
a consciousness to the environment around me
that sustains life."
—Toshi Reagon

Tools for Increasing Interdependence and Decentralization

Study Groups/Learning Community

This one seems so simple and old school, but having community to learn with is actually really crucial for human development. It means we learn to see ideas, not just through our own singular and limited perspectives, but to see how different experiences create different ways of thinking about things, of comprehending and applying ideas.

Loretta Ross teaches us that, "When people think the same idea and move in the same direction, that's a cult. When people think many different ideas and move in one direction, that's a movement."[18] Studying together with a respect for our ecosystem of ideas is movement.

I love to innovate in isolation, but when I try to exert those isolated concepts on others, I can become oppressive and controlling pretty quickly. Luckily I have good people around me who attend to or ignore me appropriately until I grow my ideas with others.

The more people who grow understanding and vision together, the more people who will feel at home in the resulting experiments. Right now we are living inside the results of

---

18   Loretta is one of the co-founders of the SisterSong Women of Color Reproductive Justice Collective, and one of the creators of the term "reproductive justice." This quote is from an interview in *The F-Word 3: A Feminist Handbook for the Revolution (Outlaw Issue)* (Oakland: PM Press, 2008).

other peoples' imaginations—people who couldn't imagine Black people being free, fat girls being sexy, disabled people being leaders. People who could only imagine their own power and dominance. When more people imagine together, and then step from imagining into thinking through the structures and protocols of a society together, then more needs are attended to. Responding to common text is a great way to do this. And it doesn't have to be just a reading group—it can be a group that watches films, listens to music, or compares experiments in changing movement practices.

I am part of many learning communities—in addition to the communities of practice I've mentioned, my generative somatics community is a learning ground. And I am currently part of an ongoing circle of facilitators studying how we create conditions in which movements can practice emergent strategy within the current dynamics of funding and non-profit structures. I learn so much every time we talk.

I also think learning circles are a great way to engage things in the broader culture that intersect with movement work and thinking. I have done a few circles and many, many events to encourage people to read and examine Octavia Butler's work from a strategic perspective, which has led to books, zines, collectives, and other tangible forms of loving Octavia.

One of my other favorite subjects of collective study has been Beyoncé. In 2014, I hosted a conference call with other social-justice-minded people about Beyoncé's self-titled visual album. In 2016, I hosted a screening of her second visual album, *Lemonade*. I have enjoyed gathering people, especially women, and especially Black women, to discuss this artist's growth in the public eye. Beyoncé is in a learning environment that is a result of her grind and her goals, but the cost includes an audience that has a low tolerance for nuance or privacy. I prefer to create spaces that are voice-to-voice or face-to-face when engaging complex conversations around things I love, given the current practice of groupthink vulture mode on the Internet.

I honor my own transformation, and I am grateful it is largely happening without a demanding audience—when I share my growth or lessons I am affirmed by my community and I keep moving.

Learning in community helps us see how our own ideas are shifting over time. Hopefully we develop and change with time, applying life experience to our way of seeing the world. It seems a sign of immaturity to hold fast to one position regardless of new information.

Grace actually spoke of this in her autobiography. For a long time she thought the most radical thing she could do was to hold tight to her political ideas.[19] And at a certain point it dawned on her that if she held one idea as conditions changed around her, her ideas would no longer be relevant. And that, in fact, the most radical thing she could do was to keep evolving her ideas as new information came her way. Community is an incredible way to get access to information you might not come across on your own.

DARCI

> "I was looking around the forest and truly grasped the importance of each plant and organism having its own role and I was reminded of how critical it is that we each play a role with our talents and strengths in movement work. I realized that some of the work my organization had been participating in was about creating uniformity. It clarified why I had felt discomfort. In simplified terms, are we training organizers to be moss when they might be canopy trees or lichen?"
> —Andrea Quijada

DARCI is a grid that allows you to organize the decisions in your group, organization, network or alliance, clarifying

---

19   Boggs, *Living for Change*.

the Decider/Delegator, and who is Accountable, Responsible, Consulted, and Informed about decisions. DARCI is the ultimate "play your position" tool. I have seen many, many versions of the DARCI tool, which was originally developed by organizational/leadership teacher Robert Gass. And dear lord it helps make things so much clearer in any group!

I have seen a lot of resistance to actually taking the time to do it. I bring it in here because when used correctly it really has the best results I have seen in clarifying work roles and decision-making structures. The investment of time on the front end saves groups from confusion and inefficient conflict later.[20]

Agenda Templates

Streamlining the iterative aspects of the work allows the bulk of organizational attention to be focused on big decisions and live work. Many groups experience meeting fatigue simply because every time they sit down, they are swirling in circles around which conversations to have, sharing too much of the wrong information and not enough of the necessary information, confused on whether they are making decisions or not.

Creating an agenda template of the most common content you cover means you have a regular structure to your time together and you can spend it on the things you are passionate about.

Examples:

Example 1: A Staff Meeting Agenda
- Check-ins
- Scheduling Updates
- Financial updates (budget, fundraising, etc.)
- Important Programmatic Content:

---

20   Here is my favorite write-up of the tool, from Social Transformation Project: http://www.stproject.org/wp-content/uploads/2014/11/darci -accountability-grid.pdf.

- news on prior decisions (brief updates of relevant news related to past decisions)
- conversation on current decisions (discussions of content that isn't ready for a decision yet)
- decision time[21] (decisions on things that have been discussed and proposed)
- Clarifying next steps, assignments, and deadlines
- Closing with gratitude/appreciation

EXAMPLE 2:
EMERGENT STRATEGY BASED GATHERING AGENDA[22]

- Welcome (honor the Land, the place, the people)
- Introductions
- Overview of Goals, Agenda, Agreements
- Framing plenary: Why Us, Here, Now?
- Emergent Session Generation (generate ideas for sessions, organize by priority and interest)
- Emergent Sessions, 1 (vote with feet, ID facilitator and note taker)
- Emergent Sessions, 2 (for each subsequent session have a quick review for extended sessions, merged sessions, new sessions or other adaptations)
- Emergent Sessions, 3
- Harvesting[23]
- Making Meaning/Closing Plenary
- Closing with appreciations to each other and to the Land

---

21 See the section in this book entitled "Efficient Consensus Decision Making" for more on this.

22 See "Emergent/Collective Agenda Development" above for details on Emergent Session Generation.

23 The World Café model works really well for harvesting. World Café involves setting up a series of small conversations that a group can cycle through, getting to build understanding through intimate conversations. Learn more at http://www.theworldcafe.com/key-concepts-resources/world-cafe-method/.

(Add more plenaries or emergent sessions as time permits, as well as game night, no/mo' talent show, local tours and other relationship-deepening activities)

Succession Planning

Yes! The horizon for your group should include leadership transitions, as well as plans for what happens if any members of the team are suddenly unavailable for any number of reasons (a movement moment requires their attention, they get sick, someone in their family gets sick, etc.). Everyone should have an exit strategy from the day they walk in.

Too many organizations suffer because they expect one person, or a core group, to stay in place forever. Some groups even lose their shape and focus trying to make everything work for one person, or a core group of people, instead of planning for succession and change.

In the longview, the whole organization should be able to imagine its own conclusion—not working to perpetuate your current structure, but rather to perpetuate justice.

Technology to Support Shared Work

Basecamp, OpenOffice, Yammer, Whatsapp, Secret Facebook groups, cel.ly, internal blogs, shared calendars— there are *a lot* of apps and resources out there to support shared work. Figure out which ones will be most helpful to you.

Transparency about who is doing what work helps the group relax. And "a relaxed body is the most powerful body."[24]

The more mysterious the work is, the less resilient the group is.

The main resistance I hear to transparency is that it takes time to get the systems in place, and that people have their own ways of managing their work. What I usually find is that people resist because they don't have systems or don't have effective systems for tracking their work. They just react

---

24   This incredible wisdom comes from Liu Hoi-man, generative somatics teacher and gifted healer.

to what's right in front of them. And they don't want others to know that. Been there, done that! That approach to life works pretty well if you are working alone and don't have any ambition. But if you are working in a group and want to have impact, eventually it will be important to create well-used systems of shared work. It's about the group being able to have enough information and contact to experience interdependence and adaptation. The key here is to do research and pick the right technology for your group, spend adequate time getting the systems started and to have a training-wheels approach for the first few months—bring it up at every meeting, really get good at using the technology as a group.

Capacity Assessment

My Ruckus coworker Megan Swoboda once had us compute the number of work hours we collectively had to apply to the upcoming year of work. We prioritized the program work we had to do and distributed our hours accordingly. This was so exciting that I now include it in most of my organizational development work.

The capacity a group has is actually a finite number—it can be measured. Maybe you're a forty hour/week type place—plan for that. And if your staff is all young people with no kids or dependents or social lives and want to do eighty to a hundred hours/week, that's fine, plan for that. But don't try to stuff the work of a hundred hours/week employee into the time of a forty hours/week employee. Same for the overall organization.

Know what your number is, and plan the work you can do within that number.

Brag and Swag Wall

At the beginning of a gathering of people after some time apart—particularly in an alliance or network setting, particularly if it's a regular meeting (annual, biannual), do a Brag and Swag Wall.

The Brag Wall can be filled up with post-it notes from

the people in the room. It should include good news and celebrations related to the work that has brought everyone together. This should also include lessons (things that could be interpreted as failures, but are lessons for the group). In my experience the most successful walls also include major personal achievements like falling in love, or a transformative breakup, or a graduation. Looks like this:

> Name
> Location/Organization
> Achievement
> Links for more information (if relevant,
>   available)

The Swag Wall can include anything the people and groups in the room created related to the central work of the gathering—t-shirts, banners, flyers, reports. So often we are doing important local work and we come together and try to share it all in words. It helps to see the ways we are speaking to our communities, the beautiful things we create.

This can be done in a half hour to two hours. As always, more time allows more stories, more depth. This can create real intimacy in a group if people are encouraged to share more than just pitches about their greatness, but share lessons.

To get really fancy, have a wall that runs the length of the space you are in and have a past, present, and future section. Let the Brag and Swag portion be in the past. Let the meeting notes accumulate as the present. Then put the next steps and agreements and decision of the meeting be the future.

I have also done events where I added a Wall of Opportunity in the future section, also populated with post-it notes, but on these post-it notes people put projects and campaigns that they want to invite people in the room to learn about and participate in. These post-its can be formatted like this:

> Name
> Location/Organization

Opportunity
Contact information to get involved

Surround yourself with your collective achievements. Let the work be tangible, and loosely linear, in a way that shows how the work builds over time.

Tools for Fractal

Personal Practice

We are always practicing something. Without intention, we are usually practicing what the dominant society wants us to practice—competing with each other to be cogs in a system that benefits the owning class, vaguely religious, vaguely patriotic. The invitation here is to "transform yourself to transform the world" inside your collective or group work. Name your personal practices to each other within your group. This may include practices around decolonizing your life; studying Black feminist thinkers; living a zero-waste existence; practices around mindfulness and spirit, body health, and exercise; focusing; organizing life, or practices around being present with friends, family. Make it so that the relationships and formations you are in are places to practice liberation.

Organizational Alignment with Vision

The vision should be a north star for an organization or group, not as a destination, but as a way of being in the world. Whatever future we have articulated that we want to create, we have to practice it in as many aspects of our current life and work as possible. This brings our vision to life. A great way to assess this is to look at how the vision shows up in various aspects of the work.

How does your collective vision show up in:
how you hire?
how you fire or transition staff?
how you handle grievances and conflict?

how and where you raise funds?

how you handle budgeting the work (is it sustainable, abundant?)?

how you make decisions (is this how you envision decisions being made? What do you need to be practicing?)?

how you provide benefits and how empowered the group feels using them?

Transformative Justice Tools

Generative Conflict Relationship Prompts

Conflict is natural between any two people. We all come from different life/family/world experiences—so even when we love each other, even when we are building movement together, we will have different opinions, different ideas on what is right. Here are some conversations that help clarify approaches to conflict and difference:

- What are our individual ways/practices of conflict?
- How did conflict happen in our families?
  - In past (romantic, familial, friend) relationships, what are the best ways we have handled conflict? And what are the worst?
  - What emotions are we most comfortable with? Least comfortable with?

How would we handle conflict and difference in our ideal world?

Specifically:

- When would we have conversations around potential tension or difference? (ASAP? During staff meetings? During a set "relationship date" time [some lovers hold a couple of hours once a week for concentrated time—babysitters, different/private space, etc.]? Before going to bed? Other?)

- Where would we have these conversations? (At the office? At a neutral location? At home? Away from home? Outdoors?)
- How would we have these conversations? (How do we want to feel during these conversations? Are there behaviors or words that would make the conversation feel unsafe or disrespectful?)
- How important is resolution to us?

A lot of times, conflict is an invitation to deepen, to learn more about each other. How do we best learn?
Possibilities:

- I learn best from reading/watching stuff and reflecting together.
- I learn best from conversation (Calm conversation? Heated conversation?).
- I learn best by being given something to reflect on, and adequate time to reflect on it.
- Other.

Finally, pay attention to what's already in motion in your pairing or group—there is a pattern in place already in most cases, understanding it will give you more agency in shifting it. Ask yourselves: What do we notice as our patterns right now?

Talking/Peace Circle

This might be one of the earliest tools ever developed by humans for deepening relationship and resolving conflict. I have participated in circles that overtly traced their methods to Indigenous peoples around the world, using a talking item to hold the sacred intention of the circle, passing it around to indicate whose turn it was to speak.

I have also been a part of circles that came together organically out of a need for people to listen to each other and be heard. I think this one is in us, and the simple act of forming a circle, a wholeness, together, then putting our truths in the center of that circle, is strengthening, clarifying, and can be healing.

The basic form is to sit in a circle with as little as possible between you (if you have a circle without a table in the middle, or without a bunch of technology and personal belongings, that helps. Clear space, a clear circle to hold whatever is spoken). Imbue an item with the power of words—the item can be an object of meaning for the group (a stone from the community garden you started), or something the group gives meaning to for the circle (in my facilitation bag, I keep a few stones and crystals—mostly turquoise and rose quartz—which have their own qualities for calming or energizing a conversation).

Ideally you can go around the circle, untimed, as many rounds as it takes to get everything spoken. If you have limited time, set a timer for each speaker, or limit the rounds. To conclude, the facilitator can ask if there are any action items based on what was heard. Most of the time, the honest words and deep listening are the only thing that is actually needed.

One note on the form: it helps to release attachment to the way things currently are, or to a singular outcome. People share differently when they are attached to an outcome that in some way involves perpetuating the current reality, such as "We have to make this relationship/organization work no matter what." I have facilitated many mediations where the first round of sharing was hampered by fear, fear that everything would fall apart, fear of a breakup or dissolution. What is true is going to continue to be true whether you say it or not—if you have a feeling that could lead to dissolution or breakup, it isn't going to disappear because you don't articulate it. But the possibility of a solution that actually works for everyone (which may include being apart!) is actually possible if everyone is honest.

Mediation 101

I think of mediation as a focusing from the talking circle model. Mediation is when two or more parties receive support from a third party to resolve a conflict. Often the third person is there to give permission for everyone to speak the truth. I love doing mediation work, and I am grateful to have been held by others through conflict in ways that have helped me understand that conflict is often a sign that there is a chance to transform.

Here are some very basic tips for mediation:

- Ideally the third person is neutral, impartial, though I have found that the more important thing is that the mediator has the discipline to create a neutral space for the mediation, regardless of their natural biases.
- Both/all people or groups in the mediation are there of their own choice. No surprises or forced mediations. If either/any party isn't ready for mediation, leave the door open for future mediation.
- Keep breathing and, as the mediator, pay attention to what's felt, not just what's said. I was in a moment of tension with a loved one recently and our mediator actually had us just feel each other, past all the words. Sometimes we talk to move away from the truth.
- "How people are in the relationship is how they will be in the break-up." My woe Jodie Tonita taught me this, and I have found it to be very useful in mediations. Not all mediations are "break-ups," but they are usually a transformation of the relationship in some way. It helps to set aside any expectation that the other party/ies will instantly transform in some way that eliminates "problematic" behavior.
- The "beef" is not always about the content that is initially brought up. The majority of mediations I have facilitated have come down to the ways people are communicating, and/or to people or organizations that feel unseen, unheard, or undervalued.
   - Sometimes, it *is* about the content that is initially brought up.

· One metaphor I use for mediation is that there is a wall, and the goal is to get on the same side of the wall, and look at it together. Sometimes to do this each side has to take turns "visiting" the other side of the wall. People may decide to stay on their side of the wall, but it helps to understand that the wall is not a forever wall, it can be crossed, circumvented, or even brought down. I will also encourage people to stop "building the wall" by looking for additional places of discontent.

· Another metaphor I use for mediation is the "river of time." I often find that people's attention is flowing along the river of time. One person or group's attention is flowing towards the past, towards what has already happened. They can't see the present, or turn towards the future. Meanwhile the other person or group's attention is flowing towards the future, and they don't understand why things can't move forward. Everyone generally thinks they are standing still, being present, in the present. Once people come into awareness of which way their attention is flowing, they have increased agency. There is usually stuff in the past that needs to be resolved to be able to look towards the future. Or their river needs to diverge into two or more channels of water. It's ok…it's all flowing towards the sea anyway.

• Have some clear agreements at the end. What happens next? There may need to be multiple mediated conversations, so create agreements about how to interact in between sessions.

  ○ As the mediator, it can be merciful to offer solid suggestions for agreements, especially if the parties are still at odds, or tender. I learned this one through error, reaching the end of a powerful mediation and then, in setting agreements, accidentally reopening all the areas of pain and difference by asking the three parties for next-step suggestions. As you are mediating, pay attention to whether these people are going to need some time apart, some space, some new boundaries, some personal practices, etc. I have learned to really trust my gut about the ideas and suggestions that come forth; there is internal synthesizing happening beyond just what we are thinking in our brain. My gut has come up with some of the most powerful next steps, things that seemed out there but really worked for the group. I think a lot of us ignore our guts, so this is another place to practice.

The Four Agreements

Basically, read Don Miguel Ruiz's *The Four Agreements: A Practical Guide to Personal Freedom*. Rooted in Toltec wisdom, I would say everything in the book is necessary for a good life and a healthy group dynamic. These are universal agreements that I have found immensely liberating for facilitating and living in an interdependent system where we hurt each other all the time:

Don't make assumptions.

Don't take things personally.

Be impeccable with your word.

Always do your best.

The book goes into detail about the why and how of these and other agreements, and all of it resonates. These agreements will change the nature of your group if lived into.

Dialectical Thinking/Humanism

"The essence of dialectical thinking is the ability to be self-critical. Being able to see that an idea you had or an activity you had engaged in which was correct at one stage can turn into its opposite at

> another stage; that whenever a person or an organization or a country is in crisis, it is necessary to look at your own concepts and be critical of them because they may have turned into traps."
> —Grace Lee Boggs

Understanding that you can be wrong, have been wrong, helps to increase the compassion needed to work through the emotional and material impacts of being wronged by another.

We often think that we must hold our position, regardless of what we learn or feel. But in fact, the opposite is true. We must learn to develop positions together, adapting to the changing conditions around us—sometimes this means we must relinquish our positions, to voice our feelings and thoughts, and hear and be influenced by, other people's opinions and information. Dialectical humanism suggests that mature humans actually need to be able to adjust beliefs and plans in the realm of changing conditions.

I know there is this idea that we grow less radical as we age, and that relinquishing radical positions is a way this manifests. This keeps people from allowing themselves to be open to their own new emotions, their new understandings. I think the truth is that, as we age, we realize the world is more complex, and we allow ourselves to get woven into that complexity. I am more radical now than I was ten years ago, although it may not look like it. I am more radical in my body, I am more radical in my clarity about the apocalyptic future and my belief that connection to each other is the most important thing to cultivate in the face of hopelessness—we don't want to cling to outdated paradigms; we want to cling to each other and shift the paradigms.

The world is changing all the time. Octavia teaches:

Why is the universe?
To shape God.
Why is God?
To shape the universe.

Facilitation Tools for Creating More Possibility

Collaborative Ideation

"I was attracted to science fiction because it was so wide open. I was able to do anything and there were no walls to hem you in and there was no human condition that you were stopped from examining."
—Octavia Butler

Ideation is just the verb for coming up with ideas. We are socialized to come up with ideas in isolation and compete with them, to have the *best* idea and get rewarded for it. But if we want a world that works for more people, we have to get into the practice of ideating together, letting others as close as possible into the intimate space where ideas are born.

My teacher Richard Strozzi-Heckler says the dream of the cell is to become two. I think the same is true of an idea—that an idea wants to be shared. And, in the sharing, it becomes more complex, more interesting, and more likely to work for more people.

Practice saying "yes" to the ideas that come from others, growing the idea with yes after yes. When you are tempted to say "no," a try asking "how?" instead. Often a "no" is a way of expressing a fear or worry that something can't work. "How?" is a collaborative question, inviting the creation process to keep going, to come up with a way for the idea to grow to the next stage.

As described above, *Octavia's Brood* leads workshops for collective sci-fi writing, which are collaborative ideation extravaganzas.[25]

---

25 You can book workshops through https://www.alliedmedia.org/octavias-brood/booking.

Low Tech/High Tech

One of the ways we reduce possibilities is by requiring a high level of technology for participation or facilitation. When it comes to community brainstorming, or a meeting, or an application, having low- and high-tech options increases the number of people who can participate.

Every workshop/meeting I facilitate can be run with just the people and a space to be in. If we have projection, speakers, options to phone in, ways to virtually broadcast, etc., yay, that's cool. But the quality of the session depends on the relationships that exist and can be built in the room.

Emergent/Collective Agenda Development

I was fortunate for many years to get to work with a brilliant man named Allen Gunn, who is on the board of The Ruckus Society. Both in that space, and in a session with Allied Media Projects, he used this method for generating the agenda for our shared time together. It was so simple and clear. I have used it in many spaces and it mostly works (when it doesn't, it's because there isn't adequate time for group process, or something is off in the composition of the group).

This can be used to generate an entire agenda, or a section of an agenda. The content generation part takes 1–1.5 hours depending on the size of the group.

Here's how it goes.

You need:

☐ A wall or floor space
☐ Post-its (scraps of paper and tape work in a pinch)
☐ Big blank paper, whiteboard, or chalkboard
☐ Writing utensils
☐ People with ideas

o Develop a skeletal structure for the agenda.[26] How many days, how many sessions, how long are the

---

26 See "Agenda Templates."

sessions, how long are the breaks and transitions, when are meals, etc.? Some tips on this:

- A good conversation between five and fifteen people needs 1.5 to two hours. Sessions where people are trying to dive deep or resolve something in thirty, forty-five minutes, even an hour, often result in frustration.
- Account for transition time: ten to fifteen minutes where people will often use the restroom, stretch, try to have phone meetings, and continue processing the content of the meeting. One of my weaknesses as a facilitator is forgetting transition times—I'm learning.

o Distribute post-its to the people.
- My usual math is that I give people the number of post-its that equals the number of sessions/conversations they can be part of. If there is time in the agenda for three periods of conversation (sessions) then I give each person three post-its.
- Ask them to write clearly and concisely a topic that they would like to discuss. It can be a declaration or a question, as long as it's clear.
- One topic per post-it.

o On the wall (or floor if there isn't enough wall space), have people put up their post-its. I prefer doing it the way Allen did, in columns across the wall, each topic getting a new column. I also sometimes do amoebic clusters, especially with groups that have a strong hierarchical tendency and can get thrown into competitive mode by something as potentially linear as columns.
- Be aware of people who can't post their own post-its and support them to place their topics up.
- The first person creates the first columns/clusters. The next person reviews what's up there and either adds their post-its to one of the existing columns/

clusters, or creates new columns/clusters.
- Invite participants to:
  - add to an existing column/cluster if it's part of the same conversation, even if the wording is different.
  - Start a new column/cluster if nothing on the wall is part of the same conversation you want to have.
- This will get chaotic for a moment as people cluster and arrange and rearrange and confer with each other. That's good; they are self organizing.
  - A less chaotic way to do this is to introduce the emergent session generating wall a few hours or days beforehand and start taking suggestions.

o Review what you have (I typically read through each column and invite the group to name each column, posting the name above the column nice and big). This takes a while, the bulk of the time. It is important to really take time to hear the longings of the room.
- As the group reviews what's on the wall, write the column heads, the big topic areas, up on a big paper/whiteboard/chalkboard. Write really neatly!

o Now, prioritize the conversations, using dotmocracy. Each person gets two votes, or three (again, I usually give people as many votes as there are sessions, with the framework that they are creating their own agenda with these votes), to prioritize which of the emerging conversations feels most important for the group to have.
- This is important—every conversation with two or more votes can be had, but you want to make sure that when you move these onto the agenda, you don't pit the top priority conversations against each other.
- Prioritizing helps the group focus in on the unique content they can cover and advance together. It

moves them away from having conversations out of a sense of obligation, and into having the conversations that are actually alive in the room.

o Once the conversations are clear and prioritized, ask for a facilitator and notetaker to volunteer for each session, and write their names up on the big paper/whiteboard/chalkboard!

o Give the group a break and move the conversations into the skeletal agenda. Voila! You have an agenda of conversations people really want to have, organized such that the top priority conversations can have good turn out.

- At the end of this process, as you begin to head to sessions, here are the people to expect to show up, and for whom you can just offer compassion and help them choose the right place to be:

    - Someone who is unhappy because they can't be in multiple/every conversation.

    - Someone who is confused. This process is new for most people and we all learn in different ways. Take time to slow it down and get clear on what is confusing for them.

    - Someone who stepped out for a phone meeting and wants to make a counter suggestion at the last minute.

    - Someone who wants to talk with you about the process instead of going to session (offer to do this later—it is a great way to learn with people, but in the moment you are usually juggling management of the sessions).

- In terms of the sessions, the goal is to articulate together the next most elegant step. That may be more conversation, or a clear action, or some research. There is always a next step. People often make the mistake of trying to create an entire work plan of what should happen. As a facilitator, keep bringing people back to the next most elegant step they can and will take, keeping it tangible and within their capacity.

- Adaptations:
  - Check in briefly between session blocks to see if there are adjustments. I used to resist adjustments because they take time, but I am growing, finding that these can really increase the group's ownership of the session and thus the outcomes. Typical adjustments include:
    » A session feels incomplete and wants to continue into the next block of time;
    » A session that seemed necessary has already been addressed and can be removed;
    » A new session has emerged, and people want to add it to the schedule.
- One last point: space matters for this. Having adequate wall space to develop the agenda is important. And having lots of options for where people do their sessions is also key—I often like to use big ballrooms or other massive spaces with lots of small conversations. Access to the outdoors also really helps!

"River Lesson: Living in a port city whose very existence has been changed and shaped by the course of a river, I've learned to listen to the water's lessons. Sitting at the water's edge, I'm reminded of the thousands of tributaries that crisscross the U.S., making their way to this rolling mass of water now flowing through the heart of New Orleans and into the Gulf of Mexico. All these streams and rivers making their way back to the source, to the goal, to the collective vision of the sea. In building our movements, we learn this: we come from different places across the country and world, we face different obstacles, paths, twists, and turns—some of us reshaping the very rocks beneath us, some of us moving the rocks with our combined strength, and some of us going around them when they can't be moved and finding another path to our desired goal. I've learned that those of us with the same dreams can find each other, and in finding each other, we can learn to move together, to build together, to shape the world together, to flow together, and maybe, just maybe…together we can reach the sea."

—Desiree Evans

OUTRO

We are almost done.

I went for a walk today—I am working on this book on a northern shore of Oahu, sitting next to the ocean all day. I went in even though it had been raining and cloudy all day, so the water was a little chilly. It felt good, it made me really alert. Then I walked down the beach, slick with salt water, rain falling on me.

While writing this book I learned I have early onset arthritis and a torn meniscus, and I have been healing. What used to be an easy walk is now an effort, balancing as the sand moves beneath my feet, leaning into the slope of beach. I was so glad my body was feeling strong enough to do this. And when I turned to walk back, I looked for my footsteps. And in spite of the effort of the walk, my footsteps were gone, smoothed by the waves—it was as if I had never walked this length of sand. My walk was both meaningful and insignificant:

This was exactly the humbling experience I needed in order to finish this book. I am putting in so much effort, wanting to get it right. But given what I know of how human creations diminish, it is most likely footsteps on the edge of the ocean of human experience. There will be a time, who knows how long, when there will be no visible trace of this work. And yet the walk happened, the work happened. It has shaped me, shaped those I am living my life with, and hopefully shaped you, dear reader. It changed the world, even if it is/was only in tiny ways that can't be seen, measured.

I could work on this book for many more years—every time I speak about emergent strategy, every time I facilitate, every time I read anything, every conversation I have shifts something in what I understand about emergence and how we can apply it to our existence and our radical work. The reason I pulled it together now, as an offering of experiential learning, is because I am excited for this conversation and these practices to keep going and growing. I have created a project called the Emergent Strategy Ideation Institute to continue this learning and sharing.[1]

I hope by now it is clear that I am not the beginning or creator of the ideas in this book, nor am I the only one thinking this way. I don't want to become a bottleneck in any way to these concepts blossoming, particularly in the realm of social justice. I want to be a good conduit.

More precisely, I want *conduit* to be a sacred role between generations, and between ways of knowing. My intention is to be a good conduit of these observations, of this wonder, to grow it. I want our generation to be a good conduit of the world we received, the life. This is why I invited so many of my teachers to share their words in this book.

I am still sitting with so many questions, questions at the scale of our species: Do we have enough time to do anything

---

1   There is another book's worth of additional content, reflections, conversation, and tools there related to emergent strategy. Check it out at alliedmedia.org/esii.

that matters? Can we do something that matters for enough people? How do we relinquish victory and loss? Can we evolve beyond a construct of constant enemies, constant crisis? Does emergence mean eventually leaving Earth—or never leaving Earth? How are we resilient during apocalypse?

What is our most compelling future? Octavia Butler showed us lots of hard futures, compelling because humans were still there, learning together. The invitation of this work is just that: let's keep learning, growing, and evolving together. Let's make the future compelling.

It feels important to end this book with an admission. It is possible that this whole book is about love. My love of this planet, my love of human beings and creatures and the idea of there being a future in which this planet is still a home to living things. My love of the humans who have taught me to be awake and to feel the world around me, and clued me in to both caring more about life and being less attached to the outcomes of life. My love of Black people and Detroit and liberation.

This is, finally, a book about the preciousness of time. It's limited and it's so sacred, friends. And everything we do, every single thought and action and relationship and institution, everything is practice ground. So practice emergent strategy, yes, but only as much as you understand that it is a way to practice love. For this, for all of this.

Soundtrack
Anohni, *Hopelessness*
Beyoncé, *Lemonade*
Bon Iver
Chance the Rapper, *Coloring Book*
Fetty Wap
Frank Ocean, *Endless/Blonde*
Gallant, *Ology* and "Blue Bucket of Gold"
Gwen Stefani, "Make Me Like You"
Hamilton: The Musical

James Blake, *The Colour of Anything*

Jazz Singer playlist featuring Nina Simone, Billie Holiday, Dinah Washington, Etta James, Sarah Vaughn, and Edith Pilaf

Jenifer Lewis, Roz Ryan, Brandy, "Ain't Nobody Got Time for That"

Kanye West, *The Life of Pablo*

Moses Sumney

Nao, "Adore You," "Like Velvet"

Prince

Rihanna, *Anti Deluxe*

Sam Dew, "Desperately"

Savages, "Adore"

Snoh Aalegra, "Emotional"

Solange, *A Seat at the Table*

St. Lucia, "Closer Than This"

THANK YOU

My family, for being my first and most constant teachers. To all my babies and nibblings, I became better with each of you.

My woes, for holding me accountable to my highest self.

My loves and lovers, for all the magic and pleasure and joy and room to grow.

Everyone who has ever worked with me in any way, for your patience.

All my teachers, for your generosity.

Sierra Pickett, Toni Moceri, and Nandi Comer for the life-saving support of my logistical life during the period of this project. And Allied Media Projects for years of growing together and for being the fiscal sponsor of all my dreams.

Charles, Suzanne, Zach, Lorna, and the entire team at AK Press for being willing to support me getting these ideas out to more people.

Thank you so much to Rachel Parsons for creating original art for the chapter pages throughout the book, and being a visual friend of emergent strategy from the very beginning. Thank you to Margaret Killjoy for getting it all on the page.

And of course, you, dear reader. Thank you for engaging with this work.

AK Press is small, in terms of staff and resources, but we also manage to be one of the world's most productive anarchist publishing houses. We publish close to twenty books every year, and distribute thousands of other titles published by like-minded independent presses and projects from around the globe. We're entirely worker-run and democratically managed. We operate without a corporate structure— no boss, no managers, no bullshit.

The Friends of AK program is a way you can directly contribute to the continued existence of AK Press, and ensure that we're able to keep publishing books like this one! Friends pay $25 a month directly into our publishing account ($30 for Canada, $35 for international), and receive a copy of every book AK Press publishes for the duration of their membership! Friends also receive a discount on anything they order from our website or buy at a table: 50% on AK titles, and 20% on everything else. We have a Friends of AK ebook program as well: $15 a month gets you an electronic copy of every book we publish for the duration of your membership. You can even sponsor a very discounted membership for someone in prison.

Email friendsofak@akpress.org for more info, or visit the Friends of AK Press website: https://www.akpress.org/friends.html

There are always great book projects in the works—so sign up now to become a Friend of AK Press, and let the presses roll!